No, Seriou Training Starts Tomorrow

The Everyman's Continuing Guide to IRONFIT Swimming, Cycling, & Running

By: Roman Mica

Edited By: Judith Houlding

This is the follow-up book to "My Training Starts Tomorrow" and it began life as the Blog: www.everymantriathlon.com

Cover Design by John Morris-Reihl

Photography: Roman Mica

raceAthlete ™ Publishing

Boulder, Colorado

www.raceArthlete.com

ISBN: 978-1-4276-2915-9

Publisher: raceAthlete ™ Publishing
4450 Arapahoe Ave
Suite 100
Boulder, Colorado 80303
www.raceAthlete.com

Cover Design: John Morris-Reihl
Photography: Roman Mica

Acknowledgments

This book is dedicated to my beautiful wife, terrific son, mother and stepfather, and all of the great friends, readers and sponsors that have made my journey from everyman to Ironman such a fantastic and thrilling ride.

I am so very grateful and thankful for all of your support and encouragement, and especially the chance to share my journey with such a caring community of endurance athletes.

Let's keep this crazy lifestyle our secret, as it surely is a great way to be alive!

Table of Contents

Chapter 1

    The Swim always comes first 7

Chapter 2

    Top Ten.. 17

Chapter 3

    The Road to Ironman Austria 41

Chapter 4

    Rant and Rave 65

Chapter 5

    Lessons learned 87

Chapter 6

    Race Reports 115

Chapter 7

    All the Gear You Need 137

Chapter 8

TRInspiration 153

Chapter 9

Long Course World Championships 169

Chapter 10

The Everyman Hat Trick ... Three races in one month........ 183

Chapter 1

The Swim Always Comes First

My first and only swim invention

All I remember is the mind-numbing tedium and the relentless boredom as I swam, staring at the same tree with every breath I took. Stroke, breath, tree...stroke, breath, tree...stroke, breath, damn bloody tree. When would I ever get past this freaking, gnarly, piss ant, God-awful tree?

Horsetooth 10 K Open Water Swim

End of Crazy Long Swim

Start of Crazy Long Swim

It started, as these things usually do, in the hot tub after a late night masters swim class.

I was just relaxing and chatting with a friend when he suggested that I should go swim the Horsetooth 10k Open Water Swim. Now that's a long swim title, but the part that I didn't seem to register at the time was the 10k bit. That's 6.2 miles long for us Yanks. A big omission.

No, Seriously, My Training Starts Tomorrow

My friend had swum the race the year before and he described it as a sort of nice and easy leisurely walk in a sun-baked park.

"Each swimmer, of course, gets their own paddler," he told me. "Your paddler makes sure you are OK and carries your food." He described in bucolic details the wonders of sipping green tea as he swam across the entire length of Horseshoe Reservoir on a warm Sunday morning.

The hot tub had just lulled me into a warm and happy and totally stupid place. So I went home, jumped online and signed up for my first and only 10k swim.

I knew I was in some serious trouble the night before the swim, when I got to the mandatory pre-race pasta dinner. Don't get me wrong. The organizers were great and the pasta was fine. It was the race program that scared the hell out of me. Scanning the list of the swimmers and their paddlers, one by one, my mouth just dropped open like some stunned bass.

These were not "serious swimmers." These were über, mega, super-duper, really, really, serious swimmers. The program listed all the racers' former accomplishments, such as the "double Channel swim". Do you know what a double Channel swim is? I bet you can guess. I did and, to my absolute horror, I guessed right.

Just so we are perfectly clear, a double Channel swim sets out across the English Channel from England to France. As the crow flies, that is about 13 miles at the point that most folks swim it, but the actual swim distance is more like 20 miles, because of the strong currents.

You drag yourself out of the cold and murky waters onto a beach in France, after hours and hours of swimming, and you say to yourself something like, "Self, have you seen the price of a train ticket through

the Chunnel to get back to England?" In lieu of reply, you turn around, jump back into the cold and murky water, and swim all the way back to jolly old England.

If you had a double Channel to your credit, you were ready for the Horsetooth 10k Open Water Swim. I, on the other hand, just sank deeper into my chair when they announced my previous swim accomplishment. My great feat of swimming was to have swum a grand total of 2.4 miles (or the length of an Ironman swim) the year before.

Oh, and did I mention that I had done this great feat of swimming in a wetsuit? And did I also forget to mention that the Horsetooth was an official masters sanctioned race, which meant that open water swim rules apply.

Which means and I'm sure I forgot to mention this, that wetsuits are strictly forbidden. However, you are allowed to grease yourself up like some old black and white movie of a swimmer from the 1920's. Why and what the grease is supposed to do remains a complete mystery to me to this day. The only greasing that I actually saw on race day was with suntan lotion.

Anyway, needless to say, my 2.4-mile great feat of swimming strength was the equivalent of falling into a pool and paddling to the other side for the double Channel experts.

I was now terrified out of my mind. The only thing that gave me comfort was my great new swim invention. You will recall that all this started in a hot tub with the promise of green tea.

My friend had informed me that you were allowed to drink and eat during the swim, but under no circumstances (remember the open water swim rules) could you touch the support boat or lake bottom. Knowing this, I had invented what I called my LDSND (Long Distance Swim Nutrition Device). It consisted of a bottle of ice tea (not green, as I'm not such a big fan) and a bottle of Gatorade, duct-taped to a swim pull buoy, which was tied to a long rope. My idea was that my support paddler could throw me the LDSND, I would happily drink and he would use the rope to pull the LDSND back to the boat.

As John Steinback noted, the best laid plans of mice and men often go awry...especially if they don't try their invention before the race. Ten minutes into the swim, I stopped and asked my paddler guy to throw me the LDSND. I unscrewed the ice tea cap and begin to (a) drink and (b) sink. In a blur of hand motion, I kept from drowning and dropped the ice tea bottle cap.

Now I had a choice. I could drink and drown, or go thirsty. Obviously I chose not to drown and thus not to drink....at least not what was now a questionable and scary mixture of ice tea and brown lake water. I let go of the LDSND, my paddler dutifully pulled it back to the boat and I resumed swimming.

The Swim Always Comes First

Long-distance swimming is an endurance event for the mind. Simply put, swimming 10k is just a few painful steps beyond mind-numbing, CSPAN-watching, grass-growing, long-ass-lecture-listening, cross-country-car-trip-through-Nebraska, international-flight-with-no-movies, brain-fryingly dull.

There's really nothing new to see, to hear, to smell, to taste, to feel, to think about, except the cold water.

I remember swimming just past the halfway point of the race and asking my paddler how much farther I had to go. He was a great older guy who had brought along a handheld GPS. Here's a hint to all you would-be open water swim support paddler types. When your swimmer asks you how much further the finish line is, just lie through your teeth. Say something like, "Oh let me check," and don't even bother to turn on the GPS as you look down at it with furrowed brow. "Well look here, it says that you have only about a quarter of a mile left to go. Just keep on swimming, Flipper."

Believe me, the last thing in the world your fragile swimmer wants to know is the painful and precise distance of 3.06 miles left to go.

The other really nasty secret of open water swimming is that it can be truly, utterly cold. I don't mean the kind of, "Please close the window, honey, I'm a bit chilly" cold. Or even that kind of, "I know I should have a much thicker sleeping bag tonight as the temperature drops" cold. The cold I'm talking about is that "I'll swim 10k when hell freezes over" type of cold. At the end of the swim I was so cold that my eyeballs had goose bumps ...and they were snug inside my goggles.

The other vivid memory I have of that day is how much I just really wanted to stop swimming. I recall swimming by a happy, frolicking family, barbecuing lunch in the sun on the beach. It took all of my mental strength not to make a sharp left turn, drag myself out of the water like some hideous, bumpy prune-creature, steal a burger and beer, plop down on the sand and tell my paddler to go meet me at the finish. Especially after I asked him how much further to the finish and he informed me that I still had 3.04 miles to go.

Ahhhhhhh!

So as not to keep you in suspense any longer, I did indeed finish the swim, in a time of about 4h 15min. The exact time really doesn't matter that much as I was at the butt end of the spear of swimmers.

As I recall, the winner finished in around 2h 20 min. If you do the math, that translates to a 1:10 per 100-yards split time. For all of you hardcore swimmers, imagin swimming a 1:10 per 100-yard pace for 10k, and you'll really understand the difference between me and a double Channel swimmer.

I just remember the wonderful relief I felt as I stumbled out of the water. And just like at the finish of an ironman, they actually have handlers who will support you as you climb out of the water …except of course that these handlers are very wet. After more than four hours of being horizontal, the body can get a bit a shaky when returning to the vertical.

I also must thank my friend Allen, who swam with me but much further ahead of me. He saved my left shoulder from the permanent damage sustained by my right shoulder. After the swim I was unable to raise my arms above my head so I took advantage of the free massage. I should have known I was in deep, deep trouble when the devil who called himself a massage therapist informed me that he did not believe in massage, but instead he used pressure and release.

The excruciating pain on my face must have been a dead giveaway to Allen as this demon from the bowels of hell twisted my right arm into a salty pretzel. Luckily, Allen noticed my tears and rescued me from further torture by saying we had to leave.

As we slowly drove back around the lake to the start and my car, in between excruciating spasms of pain darting up my spine from my right shoulder, I remember thinking to myself, 'I swam a crazy long way.'

Developing Swimmer

I finally know what I am when it comes to swimming.

I'm a developing swimmer!

It is a term the new masters coach likes to use and now so do I.

Until recently I really wasn't sure what to call myself since I took up swimming rather late in life. You know the "master swimmer" label never really seemed to fit as I did not swim in grade school, high school, or college. It seems to me that most "master swimmers" really have some sort of swimming background.

I also didn't feel very comfortable calling myself a "triathlon swimmer," as this label suggests that all I care about is swimming freestyle for as long as possible. I must confess that I really enjoy learning and swimming all of the swim strokes.

I am of course a triathlete but this does not really accurately reflect my swimming ability. So "developing swimmer" really fits the bill.

And as a developing swimmer I've come to realize that we have our own very unique and special vocabulary the best reflects or unique and special swim ability.

For instance "master swimmers" have the ability to swim at least three different speeds.

These are:

1) Easy
2) Moderate
3) Fast

Just think of these speeds on a horizontal line with easy being represented by the number 1, moderate would be represented by the number 5, and fast would obviously be represented by the number 10.

But a developing swimmer I really don't have such a wide range of speeds. In fact I only have two speeds.

1) Feasy
2) Fasy

Feasy is the speed I swim at for 90 percent of the time. It consists of a stroke that somewhat resembles the idea freestyle form but is about 90 percent slower than most masters swimmers in the pool. It does have one big advantage.: I can breathe.

The other speed lacks this essential swim technique and that's why I seldom use it.

Fasy is the speed I use when the coach says, "Swim 50 yards easy and 50 yards fast" (or 50 yards build, or 50 yards negative split, or 50 yards at a strong effort, or 50 yards over kick or 50 yards at 90 percent).

My fast speed actually consists of two speed settings. The first 25 yards or so is what you might actually consider fast. (About the speed of a motivated penguin waddle.) The second 25 yards consists of thrashing and flailing and heavy breathing, but little forward progress, (About the speed and direction of very drunk penguin.)

As a developing swimmer, I also lack another essential skill of a master swimmer, the flip turn. Don't get me wrong, I can do a flip turn … once.

After the first flip turn, events head downhill quickly. First, I completely lose any sign of an efficient swim stroke.

When I try to do a second flip turn, two things happen.

Number one: I snort up almost the entire contents of the pool.

Number two: I push off from the wall to the bottom of the pool and then bounce to the surface like a rubber basketball hit by a pissed-off NBA player.

Finally, as a developing swimmer, I swim in the lane of shame.

Why?

Because as developing swimmers we need more time to work on our stroke.

OK, the real reason is that we're much slower in our lane of shame, but that's OK, as we're just developing our swim skills ... and that why we are "developing swimmers."

Chapter 2

Top Ten

How to write a triathlon book

Since my first book (all 172 pages) was published, I have received tons of e-mails (OK, just one) asking me how I managed to write (taught a clever monkey to use keyboard and mouse) a book about the sport (death march) of triathlon.

So here are the top 10 steps you know need to know in order to write and publish a book about triathlon. Please note that you first have to have at least some triathlon experience before you can write a book, which has more than one sentence that reads, "Triathlon is a really goofy sport made up of crazy people who swim, bike, and run in the wrong order."

10) Crazy competitive friend

One day your crazy competitive friend calls you and says something like this, "Guess what…you'll never guess, so do you give up? I just entered a triathlon and guess what again? You'll never guess in a million years. I also entered you!"

I would not necessarily recommend this as a way to start your own triathlon career, but it does eliminate all the angst and worry of signing up for your first race.

9) Perform really badly in your first year of racing

The only way to write a book is to stay in the sport for a while. There is no better way to stay in the sport than to crack like a walnut in your first half-dozen races. This enables you to set the bar really low, thus almost guaranteeing that you'll do better next year.

If you almost drown in the swim, crash on the bike, and your legs lock up like vise grips on the run, you'll be assured of topping your personal best next year. This means that you can drink beer like a sailor on shore leave and still race the following year with a 100 percent chance of setting a PB (Personal Best) every time you race.

8) Make every newbie mistake in the book

The thing about writing a book is that you need to have some interesting stories to tell. Let's face it; nobody really cares about how you broke a PB by going under 14 hours in your first Ironman.

On the other hand if, for example, you happen to flat eight times in your first Ironman, you've got an interesting story to tell. So how do you flat eight times in one race?

Simple.

You break the number one rule of racing by purchasing a new bike just a few days before your Ironman.

It also helps if your race takes place just before a hurricane. This will keep the readers wondering how you actually managed to fix eight flats in such horrible conditions.

7) Computer or functional typewriter

Note to young authors: Most publishers today frown on manuscripts written in pen or pencil. Unless of course your manuscript happens to be about pens or pencils, in

Anyway, needless to say, my 2.4-mile great feat of swimming strength was the equivalent of falling into a pool and paddling to the other side for the double Channel experts.

I was now terrified out of my mind. The only thing that gave me comfort was my great new swim invention. You will recall that all this started in a hot tub with the promise of green tea.

My friend had informed me that you were allowed to drink and eat during the swim, but under no circumstances (remember the open water swim rules) could you touch the support boat or lake bottom. Knowing this, I had invented what I called my LDSND (Long Distance Swim Nutrition Device). It consisted of a bottle of ice tea (not green, as I'm not such a big fan) and a bottle of Gatorade, duct-taped to a swim pull buoy, which was tied to a long rope. My idea was that my support paddler could throw me the LDSND, I would happily drink and he would use the rope to pull the LDSND back to the boat.

As John Steinback noted, the best laid plans of mice and men often go awry...especially if they don't try their invention before the race. Ten minutes into the swim, I stopped and asked my paddler guy to throw me the LDSND. I unscrewed the ice tea cap and begin to (a) drink and (b) sink. In a blur of hand motion, I kept from drowning and dropped the ice tea bottle cap.

Now I had a choice. I could drink and drown, or go thirsty. Obviously I chose not to drown and thus not to drink....at least not what was now a questionable and scary mixture of ice tea and brown lake water. I let go of the LDSND, my paddler dutifully pulled it back to the boat and I resumed swimming.

which case it might be a clever marketing ploy.

6) The inability to spell or use proper grammar

I must confess that my complete inability to spell or put together a "classic" or "old school" sentence has been a huge help to my writing career. A manuscript full of errors gives your editor a real sense of mission and purpose.

If you submit a grammatically perfect manuscript, your editor has nothing to do but send the book to get printed. On the other hand if you are like me and have a hard time typing, let alone spelling, your editor will gleefully correct your errors while feeling great for getting the job done well.

5) Geographical Luck

It really helps to live in a place like Boulder, Colorado, or perhaps Kona on the big island of Hawaii. You can of course "right" or did he mean "write" a book about triathlon sitting at home of the farm in deepest, darkest Iowa, but it really does help to live in the Mecca of triathlon.

To be honest you can't swing a dead cat without hitting a professional triathlete in Boulder. So if you happen to be writing a book about triathlon and you have a question like, "which comes first, the run or the swim?" you'll soon discover the answer. Just walk out your front door, and ask the well-muscled, toned guy or gal who's doing a tempo run past your house.

4) Poor training discipline

If you are a hardcore triathlete, you'll never be able to write a book. You spend most of your time training or recovering from a hard workout.

But if you happen to train like me, you always have time. You can get up some crazy early hour in the morning and go for a painful track workout or you can sleep in, make yourself a big breakfast and pound away on the computer keyboard for a bit. It also helps to train a monkey to spell triathlon so you can forget about the keyboard bit and just turn on the TV.

3) Poor diet

Triathletes are meant to be lean mean endurance machines. Authors are expected to be roly-poly and perhaps "jolly" (or did I mean "jowlie") by nature? Believe me it's a lot easier to be a writer than a triathlete when it comes to your diet.

2) Blog

When you have a blog and people actually read it, you'll end up with great comments like, "I learned more from watching my dog do his duty this morning than I did reading your latest post on swimming"

Such feedback is tremendously helpful, as it gives you great ideas for the next blog post entitled, "The greyhound approach to super-fast bathroom breaks during your next race."

1) Hairy legs and a washtub belly

Everyone knows that true triathletes shave their legs and have washboard stomachs. But to really relate to your readers you must be one of them.

To know the everyman you must **be** the everyman.

That's why I have worked long and hard to resist the temptation to shave my legs. And that's also why I have worked long and hard to build up my washtub belly (OK, I got the washtub and washboard belly thing mixed up. That's my story and I'm sticking it.)

The 10 hardest obstacles to overcome to hear the words "…..you are an Ironman"

You can't deny the fact that all roads lead to an Ironman. It is after all how the sport began life. If you really consider yourself a triathlete, at some point in your life you'll get the itch to "go long." And if you happen to be of the female persuasion, chances are that like a fine wine, you'll only get better and faster with a little bit of maturity.

So for all of you who have ever had the slightest wish of racing an Ironman, here are the ten hardest obstacles to overcome (in order of difficulty) if you want to hear the words "(insert your name here,) you are an Ironman!"

10) Signing up for a race

These may seem silly but most IMs sell out in like 2.5 seconds. So if you want to race you have to be quick on the draw and sign-up the day after the race for the next year. This means that you now have a full year of training or dreading "that IM day" And please trust me when I say that one year is just way way way too long to wait. You can train for an Ironman in about three-to-four months if you have a good base.

Waiting one year is just like having a long engagement. You have one year to really consider if all those "cute" things your fiancée does, like burping the national anthem, are traits you want to spend the rest of your life with.

The same is true for an Ironman. You'll have long hours of self-doubt followed by long hours of fear, followed by long hours of dread, followed by long hours of training, followed by long hours of fear, and so on and so forth.

Sometimes I think a better strategy would be to sign-up for a race in the spring, and do it in the fall, like most sane running races.

9) The Swim

There is something about a 2.4 mile swim that just puts the fear of God into triathletes. I suspect that "something" is the very real fear of drowning.

Logically, the chances of you drowning are probably zero. But fear is not logical, so this fear looms large in many a non-swimmers psyche. (And by non-swimmer, I mean those of us who did not grow up swimming competitively.)

I'm going to only say this once:

THE SWIM IS BY FAR THE SHORTEST AND EASIEST PART OF THE RACE!

Please don't get too stressed by it. Most likely you'll be wearing a wetsuit and they'd have to mercilessly beat you over the head with sharp boat paddles to get you to sink in a wetsuit. You'll be fine and done in no time.

Fear the marathon. I really mean it. The marathon is the only unsupported (and by unsupported, I mean that unlike the swim, or the bike you have to carry your own weight) part of the race. The marathon will most likely determine your day. Be afraid...be very afraid!

8) Training or lack thereof

The really great factor about an Ironman is that you can't fudge it. There's no way, no matter how talented you are, no matter how lucky you are, no matter how fit you think you are, that you can just jump into an Ironman.

If you are like most people you'll know to exactly at what point of your race your training falter or excels. Think of training for an IM like putting dollars in the bank. Every mile you bike, run and swim is another dollar in the bank.

On race day you'll show up at that bank bright-eyed and bushy-tailed ready to withdraw all that money you saved up.

And if you've done it right, and you get 100 other things right, that money will last you through 144.6 miles. But if you are like most triathletes at some point you'll run out of cash.

And the great thing is you'll know exactly (to the minute) when this happens. And the funny thing is you'll also be able to tell on the faces of the other competitors when this happens to them. At that point your day is either done, or you are in for a very pleasant, but very long walk with a bunch of other penniless triathletes.

7) Weight or lack thereof

The average pro IM triathlete looks like a Nebraska depression-era farmer: no body fat. That's why pros are so fast. If you want to have a good IM, you'll want to be as light as possible.

It probably doesn't help you so much on the swim, but on the bike or the run, excess body weight is your enemy. I've heard it said by somebody somewhere that one pound of body weight adds something like 10 minutes per mile on the run to your time … or something like that.

One of your biggest challenges as a fit IM endurance athlete will be for you to be as light as possible on race day.

6) Time or lack thereof

I believe you can probably finish an Ironman race with as little as 10 hours of training per week, but that might be pushing it a bit. If you are an everyman triathlete, figure you'll need between 10-15 hours a week for about 3 to 4 months before the race to be race ready.

That's a lot of time to take away from your family, friends, work, television, lover, partner, dog, parents, plants, church, poker, Blog, hobbies, reading, vacation, garden, cat, football, car, sleep, and your life

5) The motion in the start of the ocean

Unlike shorter triathlons, all IMs are a mass start. There's none of this happy-go-lucky-wavy-start or, God forbid, a pool swim. Nope, it's just you and 2,000 of your not-so-best-friends. And all of them are heading like bulls in a china shop for that first buoy. And many of them are hell-bent on making it out of the water in just under an hour.

That means you'll know firsthand what it feels like to be a pair of dirty shorts in an unbalanced washing machine.

A word to the wise, watch out for the breaststrokers! These folks kick like stubborn old mules. You may get kicked in the face and perhaps get your goggles knocked of by the flutter kick, but anyone swimming the breaststroke will snap your nose like a twig and never know it.

4) Hills

It's probably true that many newbie Ironmen pick the Florida IM as their first race. That's because there is just one hill on the entire bike course, and it really isn't a hill, but just a slightly overgrown bridge overpass.

Hills are hard. And they are especially hard on a 112-mile bike ride. If you are racing a course that consists of several bike loops, the hills become especially daunting. The first time you climb them, you sprint up the hills with plenty of stamina and vigor. The second time, you grind your way up the hills with stoic determination. By the third loop, you are on a death ride to the bowels of hell.

A hill is a hill, unless you have a headwind. A headwind turns a hill into a mountain. And that's exactly what you have to look forward to, should you ever qualify for the world championships in Kona.

3) Turns

One of the more difficult races on the North American IM calendar is Wisconsin's. Not only does the bike course have plenty of hills, but the run course resembles a drunk at a drunk snake orgy.

The run course not only winds it way through the streets of Madison, up and over the football stadium, but it also up and down and around the spiral ramp of a parking garage.

And that's just in the first few miles.

There is something excruciatingly hard about making turns when you are running a marathon. The thin rubber band that is your determination can snap so easily so late in the day. Sometimes, all it takes is a hill or a sharp turn, and you find yourself walking. In Wisconsin you get plenty of both, and plenty of heat and wind make this race one of the most challenging in North America.

2) Nutrition

You can be the fittest triathlete in the world — the ultimate combination of Michael Phelps, Lance Armstrong, and Paul Tergat — you'll still crack like a walnut if you get your nutrition wrong.

It happens all the time to the best professionals in the world. During a typical race, you can burn up to 1,000 calories per hour. At the very best, if you have a strong stomach, you may be able to take in about 500 calories per hour. That leaves most triathletes with a pretty large caloric deficit at the end of the day.

Why?

From personal experience I can tell you that I can easily eat 1000 calories on a Friday night in about 2.5 minutes. That's about one super-sized whopper meal with a large leaded Coke.

But on race day on the bike, or on the run, forget about it. You'll be happy to suck down a GU or two. This is partly because you'll be too busy drinking to think about eating. On a hot day, which most race days tend to be, you'll need to drink huge amounts, plus gobble salt and electrolyte tablets just to keep from cramping and/or dehydrating.

Let me put it this way: if you've done the training, getting your nutrition right on race day is probably eighty percent of the game.

1) T2

And the #1 hardest obstacle to overcome if you want to hear the words "...you are an Ironman," is transition number 2.

By T2 you've finished two-thirds of the race. More importantly, it is now well into the day, perhaps getting toward late afternoon of early evening and you are sore, dog-tired and feeling more than a little queasy.

You roll into T2, walk into the changing tent, sit down, and a volunteer brings you some water or Gatorade. And then it hits you. You still have to run a marathon Most marathons start in the wee early morning hours of the day when people are fresh and strong. But you are neither fresh nor strong.

You have a sore butt, you are sunburned and bit dehydrated, your legs hurt, your neck hurts, your feet hurt—hell your entire body hurts, and now you have to run 26.2 miles.

If you have never run a marathon, you are at a distinct advantage because you do not yet know how much pain you'll soon feel.

If you have run a marathon, you think to yourself, "How the F am I going to do this?"

The best advice I ever got before my first IM distance race was DON'T dilly-dally in T2. So I humbly pass it on to you for that day when you finally decide you can't die without hearing the words "....you are an Ironman!"

The Ten Milestones of a Century Ride

What do you consider a long bike ride? I would say that anything over 50 miles is long, but most cyclists would say it's any distance over a century (100 miles). With that in mind, here are the ten milestones of a century bike ride.

Stage One: Anticipation and Preparation

Ah yes, the call of the open road! The night before the ride you go to bed a bit giddy. What adventures will the next day bring? Which team jersey will you wear? It has to say "I know what I'm doing," but not shout "I'm a poser who wears yellow because I saw Lance wearing it."

For women and many men, the decision is a much harder one. Not only must you color coordinate your cycling outfit, but you also must decide which shorts make your butt look smaller, and muscular, and curvaceous, and hot...all at the same time.

Stage Two: Load, Aim and Pull

You are at the start and it's way too late to back out now ... time to pull the trigger. There are hundreds of others on this century ride with you. So what's the big deal anyway? It's only 100 miles, or 160 kilometers, or about the distance that you drive to work and back 10 times over. No big whoop!

After all you did put in the training when you biked around the neighborhood for a total of something like 10 miles after work over the last two months. How hard can 100 miles really be on your new Chinese-made Exaggerator ZX-300 Crossfire Trekelo?

Stage Three: Mile 20

You've made it to the First Aid station, and you feel great. The first hour was terrific. You rode like Lance, even without the help of those wimpy "teammates." Now you get to savor a nice snack. Perhaps some chocolate chip cookies and warm orange juice. This is going to be a cakewalk. Besides, you look great in your 1997 U.S. Postal team jersey.

Stage Four: Bug Bite

Somehow a nasty black biting bug got under your jersey. Perhaps it was that old-school mesh fabric, or that swarm of flying ants you just rode through. Now this critter is going to town on the soft fleshy part of your belly. All of a sudden you complete forget how to pop out of your clips as you furiously beat at your belly. In desperation you almost tear off your jersey as the bug gives you a farewell nip and flies away.

You come to a complete stop and promptly fall over like a fresh-cut tree. Luckily, only your pride and belly are bruised, as literally hundreds of people stop and ask if you are OK.

Stage Five: The Mysterious Noise

You mount your trusty Trekelo 1000 and 1 and start to peddle. You notice a mysterious noise coming from somewhere in the bowels of the bike. It seems to only happen when you peddle, or is it only when you shift, or is it only when you brake, or it is only when you don't peddle, or is it only when you climb, or is it only when you coast down the hill? It's sort of a clicking banging, rubbing, ticking, scraping, and swooshing sound. The only thing that you know for sure is that it only gets worse the harder you listen.

Stage Six: Dry Mouth

You've made it halfway and the lush countryside around you seems to have suddenly turned into the Gobi Desert. At least that's what your mouth is telling you. No matter how much tropical-rainforest-melon-aid you drink, your mouth remains bone dry. This seems especially ironic, as just minutes ago your nose ran with the intensity of 1,000 Niagara Falls.

Stage Seven: Mirage

It's hard to believe but you made it to the finish. There's the finish line just a few feet ahead.

You are a Centuryman!

But wait! You remove your sunglasses and stare at the finish line. It turns out just to be railroad crossing with an optimistic sign that a happy third grader created which reads, "Keep Going. Only 40 more miles"

You wonder if the other cyclists around you heard that scream, or if it was just something in your head.

Stage Eight: Death March

You now watch with a sort of happy-go-lucky sadomasochism as the miles slowly, and I do mean slowly, like a snail on a Sunday crawl, slowly click by. Mile 59.........mile 59 and a quarter......mile 59 and a half.....mile 59.58. You now live for the aid stations. If you can only make it to the next one, you'll be happy.

Stage Nine: Monkey Everything

Your legs are beyond lead. Your butt stopped itching and burning long ago. Your hands and your neck have turned to mush. Your head is always down. There could be a horny rhino charging at you with the look of love in his eyes and you wouldn't see him until he mounted you. And even then you would just let him do his business, share a cigarette, and keep peddling.

All you see now is the slow, inevitable revolutions of your feet as they forever propel you down the road. Bug bites, dry mouth, mirages, death march, rhino love, it all seems like a long lifetime ago as you just keep your feet moving, one rotation at a time.

Stage Ten: The Setting Sun

Just as the sun kisses the earth, you roll across the finish line. You stop for the last time and dismount. Your legs don't work too well They want to keep cycling, and you look like a minister of funny walks. But you've done it. You've ridden 100 miles in one day.

You are a Centuryman!

A smile temporarily cross your sweat and salt-stained mouth ... that is, until you realize that you still have another five miles to ride back home because there's no one waiting to pick you up. Your partner is still at a kiddie birthday party with 20 screaming kids (and you had better not complain, either!).

Ten really important things I always forget

Recently, in Moab, I had just about two hours to contemplate the state of my current triathlon career as I ran my way down the canyon during the Canyonlands half marathon. Two hours can be a long time, especially when running hard. The nine-minute time segments between the markers go on forever with few distractions except the mounting pain, rhythmic labored breathing, and thumping heart.

So to keep my mind distracted from the growing pain of pushing my body at race pace, I mentally tallied the top ten lessons, tips, must dos and words of coaching wisdom that I frequently forget. I hope that if I share them with you , I won't forget them this year as I prepare for the2008? race season. So here are the 10 really important tips to remember, in proper triathlon order:

The Swim

10) Always, always, always look straight down.

I can't seem to help myself, but when I swim, I always catch myself looking forward or ahead. Of course this might be could be due to the normal fear of slamming headfirst into another swimmer, the wall, or the lane line. It could also be because we naturally like to see where we are going. (Expect when running. Please see number 4)

But this does not change the fact that the second the head looks forward, up, or ahead in the water, the butt sinks faster than a Japanese navy ship stomped on by Godzilla, turning me from shark boy to anchor man. Good one.

And unfortunately the converse of this rule is also always true. When swimming backstroke, I always look back and not straight up causing my butt anchor to bite, and slowing any forward motion to a sinking crawl.

9) It's all about form (as Lance Armstrong's next book could be titled)

How quickly I fall into the trap of thinking that quantity can trump quality. Sure, I go to the pool with every intention of swimming with the perfect hydrodynamic form. But all too soon my form turns to mush, and before I know it, I've swam 2,500 yards of the messiest, splashiest, floppiest, silliest, unhappiest, crappiest freestyle. I forget that 100 yards of perfect form is worth 1,000 yards of junk swimming.

8) If you can't do the time, don't do the crime

Having just said that junk yardage is a waste of time, there is really only one thing that improves my swimming, and that is … swimming.

There is really is no way (zero, nada, no how) to get good at swimming without spending long hours in the pool. So, while junk swimming may never make me a good swimmer, it does go a long way in teaching me to breath and feel comfortable in the water. As Bill Murray said in Caddyshack, "At least I've got that going for me!"

The Bike

7) Spin, spin and spin some more … no coasting

I forget to resist the temptation to push the bike. I also forget that the best thing I can do is to keep the bike in an easy gear and just spin up **and** down hills.

And I almost always forget to maintain at least 80 rpm or more.

But somehow, I never forget to throw the bike into my highest gear and really push the pace down hills, instead of using the downhill for recovery and to keep my legs moving.

6) Less is more when confronted by the dreaded monkey butt

Every year when I start biking, I inevitably end up with a raging case of monkey butt on my first couple of long rides. And every year I keep adding layers of clothing in hopes of creating a massive diaper-like barrier between me and the seat. And every year, the monkey butt goes away only when I switch to less padding. When it comes to cycling short pads, less is definitely better, as it keeps me from chafing.

5) Hills make you faster in the flats, but flats don't make you faster in the hills

On my typical ride, I tended to avoid the hills But there is no way in getting around the fact that hills build strength, muscles, and endurance, while the flats build false confidence.

The Run

4) Always, always, always look ahead when running

So why is it that when I run, I look down, and when I swim, I look ahead? How easy it is to forget to look forward and not at one's feet during the difficult parts of a run. Unlike swimming, when the head goes down on the run, the shoulders soon follow, and so does the pace. I always have to remind myself to look ahead at the horizon and my eventual goal.

3) The Roadrunner had it completely right all along

Whenever I start to push the pace I always end up increasing the length of my stride. The best, most efficient, fastest way to run quickly is to be like the Roadrunner and increase leg turnover. I forget that to go faster, all I need to do is to keep the stride length the same and just increase my turnover rate.

Beep Beep!

2) When training, resist the temptation to run fast

So I'm moving along on my long run keeping my heart rate below 140 beats per minute, when some big dude passes me, and before you know it the race is on. My heart rate spikes and I've just blown a perfectly good workout.

I always forget that the smartest and best way to get fast for endurance running is to go slowly and actually build endurance. What a concept! I need to remember to keep the speed on the track, once a week, where it belongs, or save it for my next race.

1) Use my iPod

Finally, when will I remember to bring iPod to these long races so that I don't have to play these mind games to keep myself distracted for almost two hours?

And you know what's really ironic? Maybe if I remembered all these things I would be running a half marathon so slowly. But that's another mental conversation for another time.

Beep Beep!

The "Everyman 10-step guide for every man who cannot diet" diet

So I've been thinking about this year.

To be more specific, I've been thinking about what it will really take to do actually compete and perhaps place in a race in 2008

For me the answer is painfully obvious ... I have to lose weight!

To be even that much more specific, I have to lose 20 pounds.

Why 20?

Because that gets me to an even 200 pounds, at which point I'm still racing as a Clydesdale, but as the lightest possible athlete in that category.

I am of course putting this in writing (here and now) to add a bit of public pressure to my otherwise unspoken goal.

Which immediately creates a small problem ...

A long time ago I figured out that I can't diet. Of course there is no physical reason that I can't diet. It is just that my body is weaker then my mind when it comes to resisting that extra cookie, cake or burger.

I suspect you know what I mean. The mind says "no," but the hand and mouth work lighting-fast to get the cookie in the mouth and belly before the mind can come up with a sufficient defense.

"That cookie has over 200 calories...." the mind will say, as the hands and mouth work quickly together. And then, "Mmmmm, cookie," the mind can only add as the cookie is on the fast track to the belly.

Which leaves me to once again ponder and embrace my ten-step weight loss program. In the past I have lost weight by following 10 simple rules. These are, for lack of a better term, the "Everyman 10-step guide to every man who cannot diet" diet.

Please note: I am not a dietitian nor do I play one on television. So if you follow my diet, you most certainly will end up gaining weight.

However, I do think that these are common sense steps that have worked for me in the past, at least 50 percent of the time, and hopefully they will work for both me and perhaps even you in 2008

At least we'll both have a 50 percent chance of losing weight.

More importantly, I suspect that these odds are as good as any South Beach, Jenny Craig, Weight Watchers or Atkins diet will ever give you if they were completely truthful.

So here is the "Everyman 10-step guide to every man who cannot diet" diet:

10) Brush your teeth after dinner

These are three minutes well spent. Not only is brushing your teeth after dinner great for your teeth, but just as importantly it makes your mouth feel nice and clean. You will be less likely to snack if you know that you'll be spoiling that spearmint fresh taste with a Megabox-mart bag-o-chips.

9) No snacking after dinner

No late night snacks whatsoever! When you get hungry after the late night news, just think of breakfast and how good it will taste.

8) Eat a big and healthy breakfast

I believe that most doctors would agree that a big and healthy breakfast is key the starting your day on the right foot (or so they told us in grade school). It seems to me that too often I'll just gobble up some sort of Power/Aide/Gu/Sports bar or miscellaneous refrigerator food on my way out the door. More often than not, this just sets me up for a day of snacking and overeating.

7) Eat less as the day progresses

In other words, eat a big breakfast, medium lunch, and a small dinner. I tend to do the exact opposite, which I suspect is the reason I still have that washtub–not washboard – belly.

6) Avoid trigger foods

My buddy Bolder taught me this one. I'll keep it simple and define all trigger foods as fast foods. Have you ever noticed that once you have one Big Mac or Taco Bell burrito you'll start to crave another one the next day? So in 2008 there'll be no fast food, only fast race times.

Have you ever noticed that the second you try to lose weight, your body says to you, "So that's the way it's going to be. Let me show you who really runs things around here!"

And before you know it you've put on an additional three pounds.

It is almost as if your body is screaming that it likes your current weight. "Thank you very much Mr. Mind, but please stay out of my business," it yells whenever you try to put on the eating brakes. "Oh, and by the way, you better not try to muck things up by rocking my eating boat ... or else."

It is this dynamic that makes losing weight for many of us so very difficult. The body has an internal scale and it always seems to want to return to whatever weight that scale is set on.

I believe the pros call this yo-yo-ing. It is why so many diets fail. You can lose the weight, but you just can't keep yourself at the new and lighter level for very long. Before you know it, you really start to crave junk food. And I mean, **really** crave junk food well beyond the point of just wanting a snack. The most recent studies I've read suggest that this is a real and powerful physical reaction on the part of your body, and not just weak will.

The real secret to losing weight and keeping it gone is a complete lifestyle change that resets your body's internal scale. And, by the way, dramatic weight loss (more than two pounds per week) seems to be a sure-fire way to ensure that you will yoyo back to, or well beyond, your original starting weight. It's not healthy to lose more than two pounds a week according to many dietitians.

Did I mention that I'm not a dietitian nor do I play one on TV? I have just tacked together little bits and pieces of stuff that works for me. If you would prefer to throw the advice dice here, are The Everyman Top five steps to the "Everyman 10-step guide to every man who cannot diet" diet.

5) Slow way down

I have found that when I'm very hungry I tend to eat like a ravenous wolf after a long winter of eating nothing but snow and frozen tundra. I'm beginning to suspect this is very bad for weight loss.

Have you noticed that the French have really got eating down to a culinary science? They only eat one course at a time. They won't eat until everybody at the table has gotten served, and when they do eat, the portions are very small.

They also take plenty of time to eat, and they smoke like chimneys. I may only be guessing here, but I suspect that all of this combined into one huge French eating tradition keeps them both thin, and a little stinky…from all of the smoke, of course.

4) Run like hell from anything with HFCS (High Fructose Corn Syrup)

The only good thing about high fructose corn syrup is that it acts like a canary in a coal mine. If you see the stuff on the label you are dealing with the lowest possible food denominator.

Just think of HFCS like pig slop. It is what the food industry feeds us (out of the very bottom of the slop bucket) as the cheapest and crappiest substitute for sugar they can come up with.

For instance when you go to the grocery store and you see that two-for-one deal on "genuine Italian mushroom and olive pasta sauce," just read the small print on the label. The stuff is 50 percent HFCS with a few old and stale tomatoes thrown in to make it somewhat red.

3) Exercise more and eat less

By the way that is the title of my next book. Chapter one: Exercise more

Chapter two: Eat less

That will be $16.96 please, and don't forget the $3 for shipping and handling!

2) Only one dessert per day

Now this may seem like some common sense, dim-witted advice, and I should know all about dim-witted advice, but please read on. I define dessert as anything that is mostly sugar and/or contains lots of HFCS.

With this definition in mind a can of regular Coke or Pepsi is dessert.

I also consider anything with tons of empty calories like a bag of chips as dessert. And just for the record, empty calories are those that come from simple sugars, starches, or those unhealthy fats they are banning in Chicago and New York.

The good news is that you can have the stuff that tastes good like Coke, or a Snickers bar, or a bag of Doritos, but only one "Bad Boy" per day.

If I have a bag of chips with my lunch, I cannot have a cookie for dessert. That's about as simple as I can make it for myself.

1) You must really want it!

At the end of the day, the only way I can and will lose weight is to want it more than I want the food. I need to have a realistic goal, like breaking a 2:30 Olympic distance tri time, or racing at my best possible weight, or fitting into that strapless size six dress, more than I want that cookie after lunch.

That's the Everyman 10 step guide to Everyman who cannot diet, diet. I'll let you know how I'm doing as the year goes on. Right now I just really want you to forget that one of my goals is to fit into that strapless size six dress.

Chapter 3

The Road to Ironman Austria

Signing up

I signed up for Ironman Austria in a fit of European travel glee.

It was going to be race and a vacation combined into one with my wife, my son, and my friend Michael.

First Michael dropped out. I can't blame him, as he got into Kona.

… and then there were two

Next my wife dropped out. She got a new job, so training for an IM seemed like a bit too much.

… and then there was one.

And I got to tell you, I'm way scared

I got an e-mail from the race organizers last month and it said they changed the bike course from a three-loop course to a two-loop course. I guess Austria had a bit of a reputation for being a draft fest.

The e-mail proudly proclaimed something like, "and this year we'll be going through the lovely towns of Überaberhoft instead of Oborunterhoft."

Now I don't really care if we bike through Über-this or Ober-that, but I do care about the hills. This is Austria after all, the home of the "Sound of Music." Nowhere in the e-mail did they mention the elevations of the bike course.

So I scurried my mouse over to their Web site and now I'm truly terrified of this race.

Here's the description of the swim:

"The start to the first discipline of Carinthia IRONMAN Austria occurs in the beach bath Klagenfurt, to the biggest seaside resort of Europe. During a nice bath day visit up to 15,000 guests the Klagenfurter beach bath. The 120 m long bath footbridges are created for 10,000 early birds among the spectators of the IRONMAN like and let the start area become the witch's kettle"

"10,000, eary birds, beach bath and witch's kettle." Is this the race or some kind of a strange Austrian pagan ritual?

I quickly moved on to the bike part of the race. Here's what it says about this part:

"By parties during the competition day in all distance municipalities is provided all around the whole bicycle distance for mood. After end of 180 kms it is run by the European park in the change zone."

I don't even know what this means. I couldn't make that first sentence up in my most creative or drunken mood.

So what about the run? Once again from the official Web site:

"The run distance is completely level and leads from the change zone along the north shore of the Wörthersees to the turning point to village Krumpen. After the turn it goes in the Klagenfurter city center where it is a matter like in the year before of running around the dragon in the heart of Klagenfurt."

Now this sentence actually makes some reasonable sense. I get it all except the small part about running around THE DRAGON.

Now just wait a second. There seems to be some crucial info missing. Is this a big dragon or a small dragon? Does it breathe fire at you as you run past it, or is it one of those dragons that's been asleep for a thousand years and only the kiss of a fair princess will awaken it from slumber? And if this is the case, will there be any female racers of noble birth doing the race? Because the last thing I need at the end of my marathon is some Paris Hilton-like European royal floozie locking lips with a sleeping dragon.

Now you see why I'm scared … very scared.

Just three weeks away

Reader warning: *I'm now just three weeks away from Ironman Austria and it's just like the night before finals and I'm cramming for that dreaded calculus test. Absolutely do not, I repeat…DO NOT…do any of what I'm doing if you want to lose weight and have a good race.*

In fact, just pretty much do the exact opposite of my Ironman race preparation and you'll be fine.

You've been warned.

I've been working out like a sled dog the last few weeks. I figure if you can't do the quality of work just do the quantity. For me that means early morning and late night double work-outs each day as well as the following:

1) I've given up improving on the swim. It is the best part of my race and the amount time and effort it would take to drop a minute would be monumental. So I now swim twice a week just to maintain my form and keep my skin properly chlorinated.

2) I've compressed the typical marathon four-month training plan into six weeks. This means that I'm running five days a week and putting in some pretty long runs. This could be a great way to get into quick marathon shape unless I get hurt, which is very possible. But I figure if Frank Shorter ran an average of 150 miles a week before his Olympic marathon, I can safely run 50 miles a week and still stay healthy.

3) Biking takes a lot of time that I don't really have. Ideally, you want to do at least 3 century rides (100-mile rides) before an Ironman. So I've really taken the old adage: "The hills make you stronger on the flats, but the flats don't make you stronger on the hills" to heart.

This means that I've created the (EBRE) Everyman Bike Ride Equation which is brilliant in its simplicity. It basically states that one hour hour of climbing is worth two hours of riding the flats.

In other words, you can climb for 50 miles, instead of riding the flats for 100 miles. This frees up countless hours for such things as your family or HBO.

Please note if you plan to follow the EBRE, it helps to live in Colorado. If you don't live in Colorado, you may want to consider clamping down your brakes so that they constantly rub to get the same benefit on the flats. Just budget extra money for new brakes every few weeks and stay away from any hills with such worn-out brakes.

The great thing about working out like a sled dog is that I get to eat like a sled dog. The other day I took an R & R day and treated myself to a feedbag lunch at Ruby Tuesday's.

I ordered the huge bottomless Coke and the biggest heaping plate of BBQ Ribs and fries they could bring me. More importantly I got to know the salad bar very intimately. In fact, I think that we are now official common law husband and wife.

The great thing about a salad bar is that it is only slightly healthier than the BBQ Ribs. I'm sure at one time in history (perhaps when Wendy's still had a salad bar) people actually ate lettuce (the salad kind) when they ordered a salad bar.

But let's be honest folks. Today's salad bar only has the lettuce to tease us into a healthy frame of mind. The thing is loaded with more fat and sugar than a Dairy Queen Blizzard. My "salad" bar featured heaping amounts of:

1) Bacon bits

2) Heavy syrup "fruit"

3) Nachos with fried chips

4) Mystery mayonnaise, carbohydrate, oily concoctions like pasta and potato salad

5) Assorted high calorie/salt nuts

6) Assorted high fat, oil, sugar, salt, preservative dressings
7) Mystery fried oriental crackers
8) Sour cream
9) High fat cottage cheese
10) Mystery ham and cheese
11) Iceberg lettuce

It was just wonderful. I brought back to mind those old collage days when we all put on that freshman 15, or was it 20 pounds? The boys did it by drinking way too much help-your-self-Coke, and returning to the cafeteria line over and over again for another BLT.

And the girls did it by loading up their plates at the "salad' bar to biblical proportions.

It was just this kind of heaping plate of "salad" that I now wheeled back to my table with the complimentary Ruby Tuesday's salad bar wheelbarrow to devour with that bottomless Coke.

Now some of you may rightly well wonder, what's the point of working out like a sled dog to only shovel the calories back into the body with the Ruby Tuesday's complimentary salad bar shovel?

Good point!

But I would argue, what's the point of working-out like a sled dog if you can't shovel the calories back into the body with the Ruby Tuesday's complimentary salad bar shovel?

The cherry on top to this wonderful R & R day was the ColdStone ice cream place next to the restaurant. After I finished each and every last BBQ rib I wondered over to Cold Stone and topped the meal up with a massive chocolate ice cream mixed with raspberries.

After all, they say that fruit is a healthy dessert and I just improved it with a bit of chocolate ice cream. And for those of you wondering…I did actually also finished my 9-year-ols son's ice cream as he is not yet old or wide enough to eat like a true Clydesdale.

One Week and Counting

I keep telling myself that this time next week I'll be finished with my Ironman and enjoying a very large and very Austrian wiener schnitzel and a Pilsner. But as I get ready to leave for Europe, I can't help but worry.

In a perfect world I would have made some very important and very different decision to on my road to Austria, but instead I had to make a bunch of informed compromises. I figure when life gives you lemons, peel them, chop them into little strips and make the best darn vodka martini you can.

Here are a couple of the compromises I made along my journey to get to IM Austria.

Racing with the high altitude advantage versus racing jetlagged.

Because I live in Colorado at about 6,000 feet above elevation, I enjoy the advantage of a few more red blood cells carrying extra oxygen around my body when I race at sea level. If you've never felt this high-altitude buzz at sea level, you should give it a try some day.

Basically, it feels like you can bite into the air when you walk off the plane at sea level. The air just feels so much more substantial and thick when you breathe. Running is especially rewarding, as you feel like you will never run out of air.

In fact, the racing benefits of high altitude training are one of the main reasons why so many world class runners and triathletes come to Boulder to live and train.

The newest research, however, suggest that the maxim aerobic advantage of this high altitude training lasts only a few days before your body adjusts to sea level.

So for this reason I choose to fly to Austria on Thursday (arriving Friday morning) and race on Sunday. This means that I'll still have my maximum high altitude advantage, but I'll most likely fall asleep on the bike if I get too comfortable in the aero position.

OK … The real reason I'm flying so close to the race is that I couldn't find a plane ticket to Europe for me and my family under 10 zillion dollars that won't break the bank on any day other than Thursday. It must be all those world cup fans flying back to America this week.

But let's face it, who really knows what voodoo science the airlines use to determine the ticket fare structures? Perhaps ticket prices were so high at the beginning of this week because of some celebrated and well-attended annual German/Austrian mushroom festival in Bavaria? I'll let you know if I see any suspicious mushroom hunter types on the flight over!

Quantity versus Quality of training time

Right from the beginning of training for this race, I knew that my swim would suffer. I made the conscious decision to cut back on swimming to twice a week. Swimming is by far my best event of the three.

I figured that I could swim all day, every day, and perhaps save five minutes on the swim. In an Ironman I'll probably spend five minutes in T1 just getting changed for the bike. It seemed like a waste of limited time to spend my days training for my best event.

As I'm sure you know by now the saying goes, "train your weakness and race your strength." So I did, and hopefully would.

On the other hand, I spent a lot of time riding my bike and running in the mountains. Here I also made some quality-versus-quantity compromises. If you happen to be a 40-something-year-old, married, employed, and with a child, and training for the long course world triathlon world championships, while promoting a new book, you make compromises.

This is especially true for the bike. As I'm sure you know, the bike takes the most time to train for properly. You just can't go for a one-hour bike ride three times a week and call it IM training. No, you need to ride long and far. Preferably you'll want to do at least three century rides before your next Ironman to get your body used to being on the bike for 112 miles.

I managed to squeeze in two long rides and whole bunch of half-day rides climbing up and over various local mountain passes in the Colorado high county. I figure one hour of climbing is worth two on the flats.

Am I correct? Don't know. Do you suppose the Austrians will have wiener schnitzel on the run? Mmmm! that would go would down really well with a cup of defizzed Coke and warm soup broth.

Snake Bite

I sort of just slid from the bench onto the ground.

The doctor came and asked me if I felt bad.

I felt like I was going to pass out and puke at the same time.

My son, who had just run across the finish line with me, went from tears of joy to tears of worry as they carried me into the medical tent for an IV.

But I'm getting way ahead of myself. My real Ironman Austria saga really started about 72 hours earlier and 5,000 miles away from Klagenfurt on the road to the airport with my stepfather, who asked, as we drove to the airport to catch our flight to Europe, if we had our tickets.

We did.

Did we have our passports?

We did not. Oh, merde! Scheisse! CRAP!

It was at this exact moment that my real Ironman adventure began.

But let me cut to the chase for a second before I spill the beans on what turned into the Ironman Journey of the Damned to Austria.

These three things I will remember as long as I live:

3) Running across the finish line with my family as the announcer yelled "Roman Mica...: you are an Ironman," to the hoots and hollers of a grandstand full of half- drunk Austrians. (It should be noted here that it is somewhat unusual to actually hear the words....Insert your name...you are an Ironman," as you cross the finish line, because the race announcer would have to say it about 2,500 times during a typical race. This would not only get painfully boring to the gathered crowd and pretty tiresome pretty quick for all involved.

I managed to hear those precious words. As luck would have it, I had (by sheer luck, happened to have befriended the English announcer of the race the night before!) and he remembered my tired face.

2) Completing the entire bike portion of the race with zero, zip, nada, mechanical and/or flat issues.

1) Coming back to my hotel room, running to the bathroom, opening my toiletry travel case and blissfully seeing the white and blue tube of Desitin!

I've actually done a lot of thinking about this sensitive issue the last two weeks. Perhaps too much, some of you may conclude.

However, I can tell you that after a 180-kilometer bike (the race was in Europe after all) and marathon in heat, my entire nether region was as red as a freshly boiled lobster.

This chafing problem is pretty common, but often not discussed, as it isn't "polite" for boys and girls to talk about! . So, just like the conservative right has turned "global warming" into "climate change," I now propose that we rename "raw, painful crotch rash" with a grand euphemism.

I suggest we call it a "snake bite!"

It not only sort of describes what happens when you rub something the wrong way for eight hours, but more importantly, it sounds pretty darn cool.

With this new label you can now have a very real and serious conversation with your fellow triathletes about how your race went. Here's an example:

Triathlete #1: "So, Jim, how did the Disney half-Ironman race go?"

Triathlete #2: "It went great Sandy, I kicked some Mickey butt…except that I got a really nasty snake bite on the bike."

Triathlete #1: "Ouch, I hate when that happens. I got the same thing last week."

Triathlete #2: "Wow, what a coincidence Sandy, what race did it happen at?"

Triathlete #1: "It wasn't during a race…come to think of it Jim, let's not go there. Nice weather we're having!"

But back in Boulder 72 hours before the race, I wasn't thinking about Desitin or snakebites. I was wondering how we were going to get on the plane to Europe without passports.

We quickly returned home as we could not find the passports in the car and began to tear apart the entire contents of our well prepared bags on the front lawn. It looked like a front lawn garage sale (you know when it is about noon and the garage sailors have torn into everything and you've given up trying to put it back in and sort of logical order). I guess we were lucky as this was a Thursday or somebody would have asked me how much I wanted for the bike helmet. Sadly the passports were still missing.

At this point, my well-laid plans and packing were out the window as I thought my second Ironman was about to crash and burn before my eyes.

I had made some pretty stupid travel decisions that would haunt me for the next two days. I opted to fly on Thursday for a Sunday race in Europe (remember that you lose a day traveling to the old world). This meant that we had no margin of error in our travel schedule. It also meant that I would race more or less completely jetlagged.

The latest you could check in for the race was on Saturday morning and our flight would only get us to Frankfurt on Friday afternoon. And Frankfurt is still 400 miles from Klagenfurt.

As we searched in vain for the missing passports, my stomach began to do back flips and I wondered what IM triathlon gods I had pissed off to deserve such a fate. Just as the situation looked the bleakest and we had given up making the flight and the trip, my mom suggested that we check our other car.

And guess what? All three passports winked like diamonds in the rough from the floor where they had fallen from my wife's purse. We stuffed our clothes back into the bags and jumped into my stepfather's new Toyota. I flogged it mercilessly down the highway, doing my best impression of Michael Schumacher on a tear at Monte Carlo. (That is, if Michael Schumacher drove an under-powered four cylinder blue SUV.)

We made it to the airport by the skin of our teeth. But had I known that this was only the beginning of the Journey of the Damned, I probably would have chucked the passports into the nearest garbage can and headed inside for a cold one.

Stau

The sleazy looking blonde bounded up to my car with a glimmer in her eye that suggested she was looking for more than just directions.

It was one in the morning and we had just pulled into the city center of Klagenfurt after what can only be described as the journey of the damned. We had been traveling for over 30hours and I was a bit loopy.

My son was asleep in the back of the car, but my wife simply looked up from the map and immediately assessed the situation.

"That's one eager prostitute," she said. "You better step on the gas."

My mind jumped into gear at about the same time as the car, and we sped away leaving the blonde in a cloud of diesel smoke with a forlorn look on her face.

"Welcome to Klagenfurt," I said, and wondered what sort of Ironman had come to race.

We had made it but I would never recommend this Journey of the Damned to anyone contemplating starting an Ironman in just under 30hours.

In the plane on the runway in Philadelphia waiting to takeoff to Frankfurt, the captain announced, "Just to let you know we are now 128th for takeoff, and that means we should have you in the air in about a half hour."

For my nine-year-old son I always like to break any long trip into sections. So this trip had four sections.

1) The drive from home to the airport, which was punctuated by the lost passports.
2) The flight from Denver to Philadelphia, which was uneventful.
3) The Flight from Philly to Frankfurt, which was now stalled on the runway.
4) The drive from Frankfurt to Klagenfurt, which I had idiotically estimated would take about six hours.

I looked out the window and saw what looked like rush hour in New York on the tarmac. I've never seen so many planes snaking around the airport in a dizzying line. After another half hour the captain came back on and announced, "Ladies and gentlemen we are now 123rd for takeoff, I expect to have you in the air in a half hour."

Most of the Indians on my flight smiled and shook their heads approvingly. I suspect that they must be pretty used to waiting in lines in India, as they seemed to really appreciate the captain's optimistic BS. But after the captain made this same announcement an additional three times, even they were getting a bit restless.

We did manage to take off before we ran out of fuel and before the crew had to be changed out, but nobody was happy. The crew seemed ready to throw us our (un)happy meals from the back of the plane.

What this delay meant was that we arrived in Germany in the early afternoon instead of morning. And this would have painful consequences for the last segment of the trip.

But for now I was blissfully unaware that every German in Frankfurt was busy loading up his or her car for the weekend drive down to Austria.

Instead I stood looking into the gaping maw of the oversized baggage carousel.

Nothing stirred.

All the other bags had come and departed with their owners, but my bike was nowhere to be seen. This

55

was my worst nightmare come true. I now pictured myself doing the race on a rented and rusty 10-year-old mountain bike with huge fat knobby tires.

By the way, my fear was indeed pretty real, as I happened to overhear a guy the day before the race on his cell phone begging a local bike shop to rent him something other than a mountain bike.

As I filled out the missing luggage forms, my stomach sank to a new all time low. The desk clerk informed me that most likely the bike was still in Philadelphia (bad news) but that it would arrive on tomorrow's flight (good news) and they would put it on the next flight to Klagenfurt (really good news) which would mean I'd have the bike on Sunday morning (really, really crap news, as that was race day).

My shoulders sank as I thanked him, turned around and began slowly walking out to customs. It was than that the gapping maw of the oversized baggage carousel opened, coughed, and spat out my bike. If I had left 30 seconds earlier, I would have missed my bike. They had forgotten it on the plane. I suspect the huge size and cumbersome dimensions of the massive bike box made it really hard to find.

But I was over the moon. Not only did I have my bike, but the rent-a-car guy upgraded me to a really great diesel Peugeot 407 wagon with all the bells and whistles, including a navigation system. The car was from

France with French plates, which explained two things:

1) The eagerness of the prostitute to show me her wares.

2) The navigation system only showed the topographical information on the screen. This meant that the arrow representing the car kind of just floated in space over rivers and next to lakes. I eventually checked and the car only had the street CD for France loaded in the system.

How French is that?

I can just see the selling car dealer saying, "Monsieur,why would you want to go anywhere but for France?"

The German word for traffic jam is "Stau". I know this because for the next 13NOhours I saw this sign on every autobahn in the Federal Republic. It seems that Friday afternoon is not the best time to test out the top speed of your new Mercedes on Germany's legendary speed-limitless autobahns.

I calculated that it would take us six hours to go the 600 kilometers to Klagenfurt, based on a very conservative 100 kilometers, or 60 miles, per hour.

However, it took us three hours to just get to Wurtzburg from Frankfurt which is a mere 90 Kilometers away. That meant we had averaged only 20 mph on the Autobahn for the first three hours of the trip.

By the time we arrived in Klagenfurt at 1 a.m., my right foot hurt so much from constantly pushing and releasing the accelerator pedal, that I would have been happy to pay the eager lady of the evening for a simple foot massage.

The Big Day at Last

The Bike

It was hot and getting hotter. I was just starting the second loop of the bike course when I made my biggest mistake of the race. I accidentally grabbed two bottles of sport drink instead of my usual one bottle of water and one bottle of PowerBar liquid glue.

The thermometer was now well into the nineties and I was starting to feel the heat waves coming up from the asphalt. I reached down and grabbed my water bottle and squirted some on my hands. About two minutes later I noticed that my hands felt sticky so grabbed the water bottle again and really hosed down my hands and handlebars.

I really wasn't thinking about what I was doing, because I was doing some painful math in my head.

You don't have to be Einstein to do the ugly math: Oh, this could be fun if you make it a "kid's problem" format: "If the swim takes Roman just over an hour and the first loop of the bike race takes 3 hours and 15 minutes, how much longer will the Ironman take to complete? "If the swim took me just over an hour (1:11 to be exact) and the first loop of the bike took 3:15, I was looking at around 8 to 10-hours of hot and painful racing in my very near future.(Maybe you don't like that idea (of the kiddy math problem).) "Answer: Roman was looking at about nine more hours of hot and painful racing, after two days of sleep deprivation." (or something like that)

Ironman is always like that. You go through huge physical and emotional hills and valleys. I was now in the deepest valley. The initial exuberance of the start of the race had worn off. My best event (the swim) was just a distant memory and my worst event (the run) loomed ahead like an angry cloud covered Mt. Everest. My legs were starting to feel a bit crappy and crampy, and I was very hot.

So I took my bottle of water and squirted it over my helmet and head and down my back.

It was at this exact instance that I hit the very lowest point of my race. I simultaneously realized that I had just squirted liquid glue (as I called it) all over myself because I had grabbed two bottles of this stuff at the last aide station instead of my usual bottle of water.

And realized that my helmet was now glued to my head, my hands were glued to my handlebars, and the very expensive and finely made Shimano gears in my shifters were glued to themselves.

Worse yet, the next the aid station with water was 20 kilometers down the road and the local bees had joined the party.

The good news, at least as far as my race time was concerned, was that I was now well and truly motivated to get to the next aid station as soon as humanly possible. I was like a crazed fox on a hunt determined to out run the chasing pack of hungry bees. I blew past the other competitors as if they were standing still, with the cloud of swarming bees in close pursuit. Up the hills I heard their hungry buzzing coming closer. Down the hills, I laughed out loud and yelled out to them "Catch me if you can, you Austrian mofo's bees!"

Some of the locals Austrian racers gave me an inquisitive look as I passed them, as they probably didn't know:

a) that I was being chased by the Austrian (vice) bee squad or

b) the American definition of "mofo."

Lucky the other racers were not the right demographic for American rap vids that featured such colorful terms.

And to think that it only a few hours earlier I had had one of the best swims of my life.

The Swim

The Ironman Austria swim is probably the most beautiful and unusual swims of any of the two dozen or so Ironmen around the world. The swim looks like a "P". The top round part of the "P" is in a warm, crystal clear Alpine lake surrounded by jagged mountains. The bottom line of the P is down a spectator-packed canal. It is difficult to describe what it is like swimming down a canal lined with hundreds of crazy cheering and whopping fans on both sides.

But when you are in the maelstrom of swimmers in the canal, it feels completely different. You've got racers trying to swim over and under and around you all the while you are trying to swim over and under and around them to keep them from constantly kicking you in the face.

You also have tons of the local canal water weeds that apparently have evolved specifically to wrap themselves around your neck, arms and legs as you try to swim over and under and around the guys ahead of you who are kicking you in the face.

It's sort of wet and wild version of a Three Stooges show, except that you are Curly and everybody else is slapping you around like they're Mo on a bender.

I was so relieved to get into the transition that I didn't even notice that it was a coed tent. This fact was made abundantly clear to me when I looked up from the bench I was sitting on putting on my bike shoes to behold a wet and extremely furry beaver just inches from my nose.

The owner of this untrimmed furry beast had just bent over to take remove her swimsuit. WOW, now that's not something you see, nor do you want to see, everyday.

Have they not heard of waxing in this part of the world? Perhaps Ironman Austria needs to supply the Ironwoman razor in the 2007 goodie bags.

The Run

Taking my own advice, I did not dilly-dally in T2. I sprinted out of the tent to spot my wife and son just outside transition. The next time I would see them would be in the town center where my wife sat watching the race at a local café enjoying a local brew. She would later go on to remark that this was the only way to do an Ironman.

The Austrian run course is pretty interesting in that it is basically a giant figure eight with the transition and finish areas being right in the middle of the eight. This means that you get to run around the figure eight twice.

The best part of course is the finish line, but I think the hardest thing about running a marathon during an Ironman is starting in the afternoon. For a traditional marathon you train for four months. Then, the day before, you eat a good dinner, go to bed early, have a proper breakfast, line up at the cool crack of dawn, and – bang! you go for it.

If you are like me at an Ironman, you start the marathon dead tired, hungry, sweaty, crampy, and in the middle of the hottest part of the day. You start the run knowing you are looking down a loaded double barrel shotgun of pain. That's why you never want to dilly-dally in T2 ... because if you think about the marathon just a little too much ... you'll most likely never leave the tent.

Unlike my previous race I actually felt pretty good during the first six and last six miles of the race. It was the middle part of the run that was really hard. I suspect that this has to do with what I call the TWC (Time Warp Coefficient). This every man principle states that time passes during a race in an inverse coefficient to distance to the finish.

So, for instance, the TWC on the bike means that the first 140 kilometers of the race passed by at pretty even intervals. (They put a sign at each ten kilometer mark on the course. Keep in mind that the bike part of the Ironman is 180 kilometers long.)

But it seemed to take a little longer for the 150 K marker to come up, and a lot longer for the 160 K marker. It seemed like 800 years before I got to the 170 K marker, but the last 10K just flew by.

It was the same way on the run. By the time I got to the last 10 K, or six miles point, I was like a horse that smells the hay in the barn. I felt terrific and I just flew home to the finish.

And that is the lesson I learned from doing Ironman Austria. For every painful deep dark valley you swim, bike, or run through, there will always be a glorious mountain where you feel like the king of the world. Where every heart beat is filled with the joy of life and your body surges with power and strength.

I had three simple Everyman goals for my race:

1) Finish Strong

2) Finish the bike part before the winners finishes the race

3) Finish before dark

I finished in 13:45 and met and exceed all three of these goals. At times during the race I felt like death warmed over, and at other times I felt like the king of the world.

I experienced every emotion from bitter depression to jubilant glee. But most importantly I felt incredibly alive. Every part of my body and soul ached with the knowledge of the pain and joy of life.

I suppose that why I do these races. To feel the worst and the best that being alive has to offer.

I suspect that when I'm fully recovered I'll forget the pain, go online, pick a new location to race, and close my eyes and click "submit payment" yet again.

Chapter 4

Rant and Rave

You can't win a triathlon on the swim

So I'm going to keep this rant very short and simple.

But I'm still steaming from the last "Stroke and Stride."

The Stroke and Stride is a 1500-meter swim followed by a five kilometer run. I recently had one of the worst of swims of my short S and S career.

It seems like many newbie triathletes have wrongly got it in their heads that swimming fast means swimming under, or over, or through, or on top of, other racers.

Listen up folks (and that especially means you three brain surgeons who boxed me in for a full 750 meter first loop last week): You cannot win a triathlon on the swim.

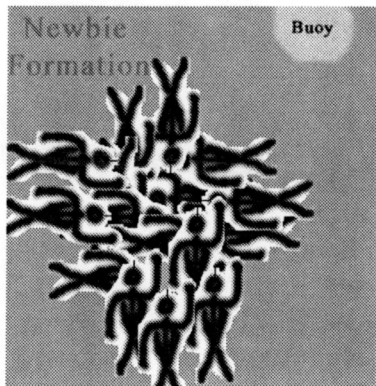

Let me repeat that so you really get it: You cannot win a triathlon on the swim!

You can **lose** a triathlon on the swim, but you'll never win the race by swimming under, or over, or through, or on top of, other racers.

To illustrate my point I've drawn a very crude sketch.

You'll notice how we were swimming last week by looking at the diagram below:

This is obviously not a good way to post a fast time.

Instead the pros will often work together on the swim.

See my crude next sketch (you'll also notice that many of the top pros have long noses as illustrated):

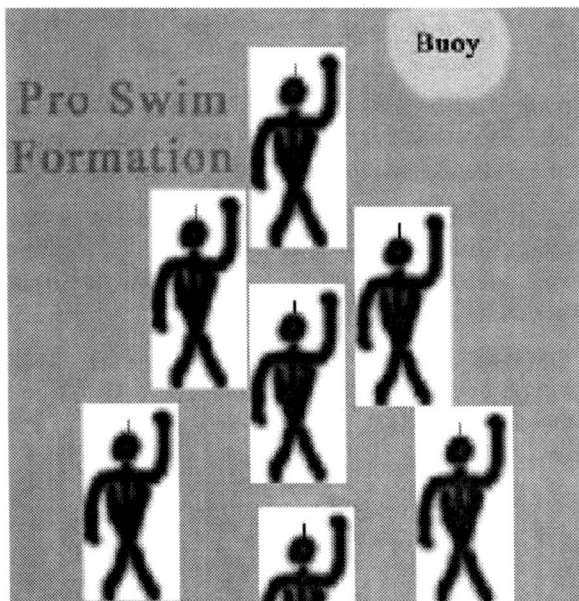

Pros will get on the toes of the leader and draft each other. This way they swim faster and come out of the water together and next to their competitors.

Why do they do this? Because they know that they you can't win the race on the swim. So for the sake of all of us, STOP swimming under, or over, or through, or on top of, other racers. You'll only go slower.

Let's be smart out there and take a page from the pro: Work together; instead of turning the swim into the heavy-duty wash cycle of your washing machine.

Sour Grapes

This is a comment from Dave Miller about my recent swim rant:

"Sounds like sour grapes to me. The people swimming over you most likely are not newbies, but faster, more experienced swimmers wishing you would get out of their way," His comment got me to click on Photoshop and go at it for a few more illustrative graphics.

You may want to stop reading right about here because my graphic talents are not even equal to that of my young son. As proof, I offer up a recent drawing of his. So I would highly suggest that you just skip to the next chapter to a nice story that includes no Photoshop graphics whatsoever.

You've been warned!

This is the text of the email I just sent Dave: "Thanks for your comment. Sour Grapes? ...no, not really. Actually I got boxed in by a group of swimmers of similar ability. I should have gone anaerobic and swum ahead of them, but I didn't think about that as I was swimming.

I just kept wondering why they kept slamming into me instead of swimming in clear water."

To illustrate this point I've drawn another terrible graphic. You will notice that I'm red as a lobster because I'm steamed from being boxed in.

You will also notice that the real problem is not with the newbies. The problem is the newbies who's been swimming a year or two and now decides that she/he is the next Phelps or Spitz. These are the boys and gals who like to swim under, or over, or through, or on top of, other racers.

I think that true newbies tend to be a little too intimidated on the swim to really go and mix it up in the "crunch."

You'll notice in the next awful graphic that I define the crunch as the area where everybody comes together as they head for the first buoy. It is the narrowest part of the funnel that forces swimmers (who all started pretty far apart) to come together.

So if you look at the diagram carefully, you'll also notice that the worst possible place to start the race (if you are a slower newbie swimmer) is in a direct straight line with the first buoy.

Why?

Because everybody else in the entire race will eventually move into your swim line and you'll be the person caught in the crunch. That's why many coaches will advise newbies to start on the outside to keep out of the crunch zone as long as possible.

But no matter where you start, at some point you will end up in your own crunch zone. That is just what happens when you put several hundred or thousand

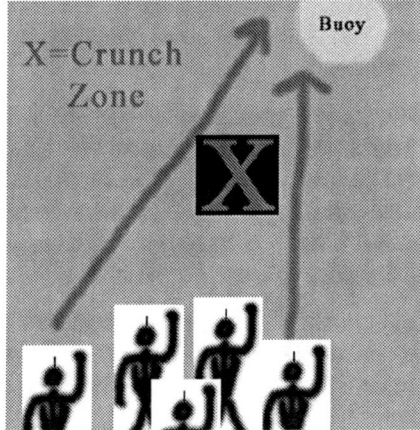

swimmers into any given body of water and pull ther trigger. In Austria I was drafting a good swimmer when I noticed that we were going to completely miss going around one of the buoys. We were in fact swimming right for a course marshal who was turning folks around to head back around the buoy.

I felt like I owed my drafting partner a heads-up on the situation so I sort of tapped his shoulder. He just kept on swimming. So I grabbed him by the waist (bad idea!) to get his attention. He spun around in the water like an angry python and raised his fist to clobber me on the nose. It wasn't until I pointed to the buoy that he understood and thanked me for stopping him.

Sometimes we all get a little too caught up in the moment and do stupid things in the heat of battle. That's why I always try to remind before every race that you can't win a triathlon on the swim.

Oh yeah ... I promise no more pitiful illustrations.

New Tri Rules

You can't call yourself a cutting edge high-tech tri apparel company if you still sew labels into your clothing.

The other day I bought new tri shorts from a well known brand that came with a clothing tag the size of a snow shovel. The tag explained how the shorts were made from this space-age material using the latest in ultra-dry, ultra-cool, ultra-expensive nanotechnology.

Except that about two minutes into my first run in the new shorts, the razor sharp label stabbed itself into my back like Jack the Ripper on a Friday night in London.

Do the sports clothing companies actually test their apparel on real athletes, or do they just have the marketing weasels come up with "ultra this" and "ultra that" wording?

I'm betting on the marketing weasels, as I've been spending a lot of time cutting labels out of my "so-called" high performance endurance apparel.

Triathletes must stop calling their Cervelo Sorrento, Bosso, and so on "Bike Porn."

Boys, boys, boys perhaps you need to Google the term "Porn" and see what a real woman looks like.

While a bike may be somewhat curvy and desirable, I would suggest that you try taking it to dinner, plying it with expensive wine and caviar, and escorting it up to bed. Once you have it in bed, try doing those things that would make your mother blush and you'll soon realize why describing a bike as being pornographic is like French kissing your poodle.

Harvard must educate an entire new crop of running shoe scientists.

Do you pronate or supinate or incubate? Clearly the only real science behind today's running shoes goes into predicting the hottest color for next year.

For the longest time every running shoe company worked to develop the best shoe to pad, control, enhance, regulate, and support our "unnatural" tendency to pronate or suplinate when we run. That is, until about a year ago when Nike came out with their new shoe called the "Free," which promises to build up your feet and muscles by providing zero support.

So what is the theory du jour? Complete support or zero support? Why don't you call me when you actually apply some real science to the problem instead of spending your research budget on sponsoring the tallest basketball player with the most gold around his neck!

Male professionals must stop wearing the man bra when they race.

The Man Bra: it was very funny on Seinfeld when George's dad suggested selling it as a wacky business plan. But who would have known that today's top male professionals would actually wear the damn thing while racing.

I don't care how fit you are boys, but you should know that the man bra is about as attractive as bike porn.

Women professionals must start wearing a "g string" bikini when they race.

Look gals you are so close to wearing it already, why not pull the trigger and go all the way? The bottoms you already wear are just a snip or two away from being a "g string" anyway, so just go for it. Imagine how much cooler your butt would be in a ultra-high tech space age race bottom. Now that's the kind of nanotechnology that we all need to support.

The Eighth Lemming

I have this theory that at any given time I can only remember seven technical procedures at the same time. You know like changing the clock in my car, or programming my VCR or DVR, or swapping out the screen saver on my computer.

The second I learn the eighth technical procedure, like how to set my cell phone from ring to vibrate, the very first procedure in line falls off the cliff into the ocean of forgotten crap.

So it was with a mixture of dread and trepidation that I, along with a friend, set out to install the newish Cateye wireless computer on my wife's bike.

Now I really only need or want about four readouts from my bike computer:

1) Speed
2) Time
3) Distance
4) Tire pressure

Of course nobody makes a bike computer that tells you tire pressure but wouldn't it be a cool and useful feature to have on your bike? (I hope all you Cateye executives are paying attention here because a) that's my great and free suggestion to you and b) I'm about to tear you a new one.)

Unlike me, my wife also really likes to know her peddle rpm (or peddle cadence as some of you may call it). And since I hate wires, I shelled out well over $100 U.S. smackaroos for the Cateye wireless bike computer that also measures paddle cadence.

This little monster has something like 4,000 buttons and 15 different readouts on 20 different screens.

To install it you will first need an artist painting stand. When you open the box you'll be amazed to find this tiny folded piece of rice paper that folds out into a city-map-sized directions manual. And just to be clear here, the scale on this foldout direction map would be about 1 to 1.

Once you unfold this treasure of origami, you'll need the painter's stand to display these massive directions that come in every language including Swahili and several dialects of Latvian.

Anyway, once you locate the Queen's English you will immediate be directed over to read the car owner's manual sized instruction book that comes along with this beast of a bike computer. And when I say car owner's manual, I'm including all those other warranty books and mystery pamphlets that come packaged with the car manual that nobody reads.

Once again you have to locate the Queen's English in this baby Bible. Once you locate the correct section the fun really begins. The manual explains that you have to press a serious of buttons in a very specific order to get the sending unit and the receiving (head) unit talking to each other.

It took us about one hour to acquaint these two parts. Somehow we did it by a) pressing the bottoms in a completely random order, followed by waving a dead chicken in the air all the while reciting the pledge backwards, and promising to name our second born "Cateye."

I suggest that if you buy this particular bike computer you also make a quick stop at the grocery store on the way home to purchase your dead chicken. It will save you a trip, plus make a tasty meal after hours of futile effort to properly install this device.

Anyway, we now had the two units talking to each other, so we installed them on the bike. This process took about two painless minutes and I was ready to declare victory and get my wife's satisfied admiration.

That's when my friend noticed that the computer was displaying the speed and distance in kilometers.

This is a problem, since we live in the U.S. and are bit set on the mile. If I had only known that it would be much easier to ascend Everest than change the Cateye to display miles, I may have spent the next several hours trying on crampons. Instead we dove into the abyss only to discover that this very expensive bike computer has so many functions as to even confound Einstein.

For instance, and I'm pretty sure about this, the eleventh screen (you can scroll through screens like on a cell phone) can be used to recalculate third world debt.

The twelfth screen, and I'm almost certain about this, is used locally by NCAR (National Center for Atmospheric Research) to analyze world weather patterns in the year 2080.

The fifteenth screen, and here I'm totally guessing, will calculate the number of drops of water in Lake Michigan, if one drop equals one rotation of the front wheel, divided by your rpm while coasting down a 12 percent grade.

After many long hours of studying the Swahili section of the owner's manual, and hitting every button in every possible combination, we happened to switch it over to miles when I accidentally dropped it from my tired and clammy hands.

* Post Script: My wife has now used the Cateye on several rides and she has yet to figure out how to

reset it. I keep suggesting that she drop it into the garbage with enough force to teach it who's boss.

6 Reason why people hate triathletes

Let's face it folks, we are hated. Most of our friends think we are completely crazy. The rest of the world says a huge collective, "And why would you want to do that?" when you tell them the swim, bike, run distances in an Ironman.

What's worse is after a short amount of time of getting to know us, many "normal" (or as I will call them non-athletes) develop a passionate loathing for triathletes. Why? Here are a few of my personal observations.

6) Bald Legs

You have to admit, most non-athlete women and men like men's legs the way God made them, pasty and furry. I will confess here and now that I completely sympathize with these folks.

I recall a distant time in my past when I was college and my roommate took up with the local bike team. It was bad enough that he ate all the cereal in our place at weird times of the night like 2 a.m., but then he started to shave his legs.

Let me cut to the chase. Living with a guy who shaves his legs is like having a girlfriend with all the downside of constant grooming, and none of the up side.

Plus, he would spend hours in the shower either

a) showering before a ride or
b) showering after a ride or
c) shaving his legs.

This meant that our limited hot water lasted about one leg … which for me meant that I quickly got used to taking very cold and very furry showers.

5) Ironman Tattoos

There's nothing that says you are an elite athlete quite like having the brand of a company forever branded on your body. I'm sure like me, many non athletes certainly use fine corporate products and services daily, but the thought of tattooing themselves with a corporate logo of their manufacturer is a bit much. Can you image the conversation with your spouse? "Honey the dishwasher does such a great job that I just added a Whirlpool tattoo to my left shoulder."

"That's great dear; it just looks super above your Volvo and American Express tattoos. I'm getting my Playtex tattoo done tomorrow."

4) Triathlon Talk

Have you ever been to an all triathlete party? I have, and the conversation can be pretty dull. It tends to go something like this:

Triathlete 1: So how you doing today?

Triathlete 2: I'm pretty tired as a I just swam after my recovery run.

Triathlete1: How far did you run?

Triathlete 2: I ran easy 5 miles today, but I ran 17 yesterday.

Triathlete 1: Yeah, I know what you mean, I just biked 70 miles and I'm a bit tired as well.

Triathlete 2: Yup.

Triathlete 1: Yup. I think I'll go home and take a nap.

Not only is the conversation dull, but only a triathlete would consider recovering from a 17-mile run with another run. Many people would consider a 17 mile run a great accomplishment, but for a triathlete it's just another day training.

3) Weird Food

When you really think about it we really eat some strange food. To the average non-athlete, our diets are about as normal as captive baby seals ... which, by the way, eat a constant diet of vitamin-stuffed ground up mullet.

Here's just a small sample of the stuff we consume on a regular basic. MAX, ADE, OX, GU, BOOM, GEL. Consider the sheer amount of bewildering performance enhancing drinks and supplements we buy and eat. They have one thing in common: a fluorescent Day-Glo color. Personally I tend to judge them by the stickiness factor. The more they make my hands stick to the handlebars of my bike, the better they must be.

2) Monkey Butt

So in nature a female monkey signals her readiness for immediate coitus by displaying her huge red swollen behind.

The average triathlete at best is sending mixed signals after a long bike ride or run. It took me about a year to discover the joys of lubrication. The leg pain after a marathon is nothing compared to the searing pain of taking a shower with raw nipples. However, nothing identifies a triathlete, or a horny monkey, like a raging case of monkey butt after an especially long session on the bike.

It is no wonder that non athletes get so easily confused by our mixed signals. Are we ready for love or just a Costco-size tube of Desitin diaper rash cream?

1) Workout Wear

I'm not making this up, but I know a guy who now exclusively wears Drifit all the time, everywhere he goes, for every occasion under the sun.

If it was possible to wear a Nike tuxedo, or perhaps a Nike wedding dress I'm sure that he and his girlfriend would be the first at the altar with Drifit everything, sporting running shoes, watch, sunglasses, socks, sports bra, underwear and condom.

Can you blame the average non athlete for getting hot around the collar when we seem to always be either going to, or coming from the gym?

Things that make me smile

All too often when I'm training I have a scowl on my face. This could be because, like this morning, I got up to run at a time when most sane people are still comfortably cuddled in their comfy beds. Or it could be because I'm pushing the pace beyond my normal comfort zone of an easy to moderate stroll. So I've come to really cherish those moments that make me smile. Here are just a few examples:

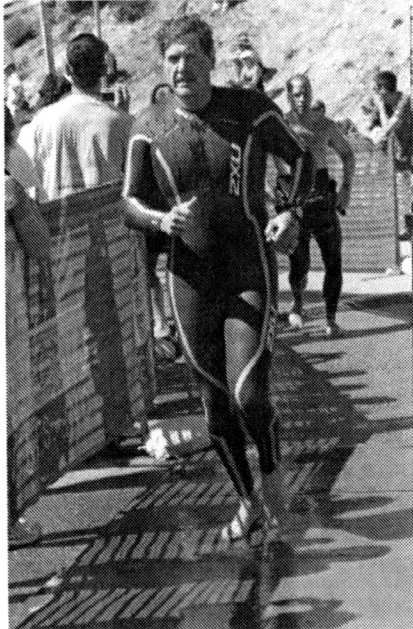

Cars that cross the centerline when they pass me:

Whether I'm running or biking I always get a huge smile on my face when a car comes up from behind and actually crosses the center line to pass me. This not only makes me smile, but it makes me giddy with glee as this thoughtful move from the mysterious driver gives me enough room on my side of the road to feel safe and secure.

Thank you, mystery drivers, for being so considerate and thoughtful!

I sincerely appreciate your small but kind act. I hope someday, when you are out on the open road running or cycling, the idiot driver that scares the hell out of you by almost rubbing his or her side mirror against your elbow (even though there are no other cars within miles) gets a flat tire on a truck clogged highway with no shoulder and no cell phone coverage. Let's see how you like it when something like an eighteen wheeler that weights 1000 times more than them decides to play a cruel game of chicken.

Cyclists who stop and ask if you need help when you breakdown:

I'm so grateful to all of you great roadies, triathletes, and weekend warriors who stop and ask a stranded cyclist if he or she needs help. There are very few things that bring on that sinking feeling in my stomach faster having a mechanical breakdown or flat miles away from home. I'm usually tired and not really prepared for the changing weather when something bad breaks on my bike. And by bad I mean anything really. It is comforting to know that I'm not all alone out in the middle of nowhere.

And even if I can easily fix the flat, it makes me smile from one ear to the other when another cyclist stops and says, "Are you Ok?" or "Do you need a hand?" I'm OK, but thanks for watching out for my back.

Non-elitist/purist Triathletes

In two weeks I'm racing a small little local triathlon that includes a 500-yard pool swim. I always smile inside when I tell somebody I'll be doing the Longmont triathlon and they don't look at me like I'm some rank amateur because I'm doing a triathlon with a "pool swim." All too often I hear these words, "I don't do race with a pool swim," or the opposite "I don't do open water swims." Can we all just all please agree that as long as water is involved somehow or someway (be that in a pool, lake, ocean, river or enormous hot tub) it is indeed a triathlon.

Water = Triathlon

No water = Duathlon

It really is that simple, so let's not get all hung up about what holds the water. I really respect anyone who races a triathlon no matter how long or short of swim. There is just something special (it makes me smile) about starting a race with a swim instead of a run.

Encouraging words when being passed

It never does get old. Whenever somebody passes me on the bike or on the run and they say a few kind words of encouragement like, "You are going great," or "keep up the good work," I smile like an idiot, because I know that somebody else who is probably working harder than me has taken the time and energy to help me succeed.

You've got to love that!

It's a kind of unwritten bond that says to me, "We're all in this race together, and while we may be competing, I still want to see you do well."

Swimmers who know the basic rules of masters swimming

We have a guy at my masters class who shall remain nameless (actually I don't know his real name) but who has earned the nickname "The Professional." He has earned that nickname because he considers himself a professional on all matters of novice, masters, collegiate, world class, Olympic and even kiddie swimming. He tends to enter the water like many of the former college swimmers do, by running to the edge of the lane, jumping in feet first, and immediately swimming at a ferocious pace to the other end of the pool.

Except that unlike the professional, all of the former college swimmers do not do this when I'm swimming toward then in the same lane as they bound into the water. The other day the professional almost jumped right on top of my head. It almost literally scared the piss out of me. It took a feat of super human pee control to keep me from polluting the pool.

So now I just smile when a non-professional swimmer simple slides into the water and asks me if I wouldn't mind sharing my lane.

Triathletes who know how to close a wet suit and leash

Ok, I admit that this may be something that is unique to me but it does make me smile. For the first time at my last race somebody actually knew how to close the flap at the top of my wet suit. As you may know it is almost impossible to close the top part of the wet suit (the flap that covers the zipper) by yourself. You need to have a nearby triathlete do it for you as you are about to start the race. Most triathletes don't zip the wet suit until the very start of the race, as they would quickly sizzle in the suit. However it seems that most triathletes are at a complete loss as to the proper way to close a wet suit and leash. To my way of thinking there is only one proper technique. The following are problematic methods to zip close the wet suit and leash:

#1 Crazed Killer Phython Method

Velcro the top zipper flap closed and leave leash unattached and hanging down and tangling from the zipper. In this common scenario the leash will inevitably wrap itself around my neck when I begin to swim and try to choke me like a crazed python. I'll spend at least half of the swim trying to unwrap the cagey leash from my neck.

#2 Wetsuit Love Hickey Method

Velcro the top zipper flap closed with leash end sticking out of the top of the flap. This is another common method that people use that drives me crazy. With the leash end under the flap but sticking out of the top, I always end up with a huge red wetsuit love hickey kiss on the back of my neck. The top of the leash rubs against the back of my neck when I swim to such an extent that my wife thinks I've been making out with an octopus.

#3 Cagey Hide and Seek Leash Method

Velcro the leash under the flap but from the top instead of from the bottom. In this problematic method my friendly race-day-neighbor zips up my wet suit and takes the end of the leash and Velcros it under the flap with the end stuck under the top of the flap. This creates a sort of giant "O" out of the leash as the ends stick under the flap from the top instead of the bottom of the flap. The result of this method is that not only will I end up with a wetsuit hickey, but also the giant O leash is almost impossible to grab and pull at the end of the swim. It always seems to deafly defy my probing hands as I try to grab the leash to unzip the wet suit.

#4 The Everyman Recommended Method

The only method that I find works for me is when the leash is closed under the flap from the bottom of the flap creating a sort of U with the leash. And when somebody actually does this for me I smile, and smile, and smile.

Newbies

Newbies always make me smile because you are the future of the sport. You guys read my grammatically challenged ramblings and you make me feel smart and in the know ... which is something that always makes me smile.

So, thank you, newbies, for giving this crazy sport a whirl. You guys are great and I hope that if I ever have the chance to actually pass you in a race I'll say a few words of encouragement like "you are doing great" and hopefully put a smile on your face.

Chapter 5

Lessons Learned

Top ten ways to suck at your next triathlon

Just to keep it honest, I must admit that I have countless years of experience at sucking come race day. So please note that these Top Ten Tips don't just come from your average Joe DNF. No they don't! Indeed, if they offered a technical degree in RDS (Race Day Suckage), I would be not only be the student, but the professor, dean and trustee of the USDS (The University of Race Day Suckage)

10. Try something crazy and few just minutes before the race

Here's a real life example. For instance if you really want to suck, I would recommend that you try switching your trusted and true traditional pre-race meal of PB and J on a bagel to something like a bowl of red sugar-bomb cereal with plenty of milk. Now you want to be sure to top up your stomach with a 20 ounce bottle of blue Gatorade just minutes before you PR half marathon attempt. The swishing and swirling combination of white dairy, with red sugar bomb cereal, and blue Gatorade as you run make for the most patriotic and explosive display of Fourth of July holiday hurling your fellow racers will ever witness.

The magnificent pageantry of watching you collapse at mile five after this patriotic display of exploding colors coming from every orifice in your body will make even the biggest fireworks display seem boring and lame in comparison. You've never seen a more magnificent Roman candle unless you happened to be at mile five with me a few years ago when the soldiers running the race all but saluted this real life exploding Roman candle.

9. One word: "Tequila"

A lot of time, effort, and science has been conducted in trying to research the perfect before, during, and after race hydration. But if you really want to suck with the best of them you need only one drink to help you maximize your suckage potential, and that drink comes from the distilled sap from hearts of the agave plant. To many of us that drink is more commonly known as tequila. As a bonus, tequila has wonderful natural properties that enhance suckage beyond that of most other alcoholic libation.

Tequila has the wonderful ability to completely dehydrate you the night before a big race. After a night of drinking tequila, this property when combined with its slight hallucinogenic effect of the distilled agave plant, makes for a guaranteed PW (Personal Worst) at any big race.

Yes, you'll be sure to go into the race as dry as the Sahara and as Goofy as any Walt Disney character. You won't know even when to swim, bike, or run, so may just decide that a swim would be better after a long bike and run, instead of before. Besides ... , why would you want to get in the water when you are already over hydrated on tequila.

8. Whim

If you really want to be in the race day Suckage Hall of Fame like me, you may want to let "whim" be your guide.

For instance I know of a former professional short course triathlete (who shall remain nameless but forever embarrassed) who, as well, had never run a marathon in his life. He was visiting a friend in the southwest part of our country who happened to mention that he was running a marathon over the weekend and asked this nameless pro if he wanted to join him.

On a whim the nameless and not-yet-embarrassed pro said, "Sure!" Now, keep in mind that he had not only never run a marathon, had never trained for a marathon, but more importantly had not even brought his running shoes with him on this visit.

So on a whim (there is that word again) he decided to borrow his friend's running shoes and go for it. Except of course that his friend's running shoes were a bit too small, or a bit too big, or a bit too yellow. The exact details of the shoes are not important beyond the fact that they were not this professionals personal shoes, and they certainly did not fit him well.

So on the day of the marathon this soon-to-be-embarrassed pro lined up on starting line on a whim with no training, no goals, no experience at the marathon distance and with shoes that did not fit well. He of course smashed all expectations and ran a marathon so fast that many of us would give our first and last born to ever be able to run such a fine and fast race with training, experience and goals.

That part did not suck, but the fact that he literally could not walk for the next week…really did!

7. Bet Big…Loose Big

I like to bet every so often. In fact when race day comes, I'll bet that we are all betting on something, whether we know it or not. For instance some of us are betting that weather will be cold, while other are betting that it will be hot, while most of us are betting that it will be just right.

We also bet with our training. Some of us bet that we'll only need to swim a little in training since the swim is the shortest part of the race. Others are betting that we'll be able to make up any time lost time on the bike by having an incredible run. While still other of us are betting that we'll be able to tear it up on the bike, so the run won't be as important to our finish time.

We also bet on our nutrition and on even our mechanical skills. I've seen more than one triathlete call it a day after they had a flat on the bike. They bet that they would not flat by not preparing (or even knowing how to change a flat tire). When they did flat, they lost the bet and were forced out of the race.

But every-so-often, when the stars are aligned just right and the moon is in the perfect place in the heavens, we have that perfect storm of a race when all of our bets go south. Yes, every single bet we placed gets trumped, or gets called as a bluff, or comes up snake eyes.

This famously happened to me in Ogden, Utah, when I decided to run the Top of Utah marathon that is billed as being very fast and mostly downhill. In fact the first 20 miles or so are almost completely downhill through a lovely canyon that is supposed to be wonderfully shady and cool. I placed two big bets that day:

The weather would be cool. We arrived at start of the marathon at 6 a.m. on the top of a mountain and it was already 80 plus degrees ... Snake eyes.

2) The course would be fast enough to qualify for Boston. And indeed I ran the fasted half-marathon of my life, but by mile 18, my quads were so fried from the constant downhill pounding that they turned to

noodles at mile 20. Somehow I managed to crawl across the finish line in temperatures approaching 100 degrees for a magnificent new PW.

6. Race on Tubular tires, also known as "sew-ups"

When I was a young buck in college I actually got into a bit of serious cycling and raced for a while. It wasn't long before I realized that all of the fast guys rode on tubular tires. Tubbies, as I like to call them, differ from clinchers in that they don't have beads. Instead, the two edges of the tire are sewn together around the inner tube. Tubulars are used on special rims, and are held on to the rims by glue. Tubulars used to be fairly common on high-performance bicycles, but these days they are an endangered species on most bikes.

However there is still an "Old School" hardcore group of athletes that swear by them. They point to the fact that the pros on tour ride them as well as the top triathletes at Kona. They say they are faster because they can be pumped up to a higher pressure, and that they handle better. This is all well and true until you flat.

You may recall the famous moment from a few years ago during the Kona Ironman World Championships when Norman Stadler threw his bike around like a used tissue after his second flat. Why? Because he couldn't remove his tubular tire from his rim.

Tubular tire are almost impossible to change in a race situation. That's part of the reason the boys on the tour don't change them. They just swap wheels.

Worse yet, if you actually do manage to change a tubular tire while racing, you'll live the rest of the race in constant terror. Back in the day when I raced, I had a tubular roll off the rim on a sharp bend. It was bloody hot and the glue that holds the tire to the rim got soft and let go. I spent the next two weeks silently screaming in the shower whenever the water hit my tapestry of road rash.

If you truly want to save seconds by riding tubular like a pro, you better be prepared to crash like a pro and/or throw your bike around in disgust with the best of the best.

5. Under Training

This is a discipline that I tend to excel at as race day nears. Just like the cheetah of the African Serengeti, I like to rely on muscle memory to get my through a race.

Please note that I have a very long and exceptional muscle memory. This means that sometimes I go days and even weeks without training the run, bike, or swim. So on race day as I'm waiting for the swim to start I'm left with only relying on that one long workout that I did several weeks ago to get me through the race.

Fortunately the results are of course predictable. I end up walking the run. Which, to a lot of you, may seem like a bad thing but until you've walked a few runs you don't really know how much fun it really is at the back of the bus...or in this case, at the back of the run.

While all of you speedy types are huffing and puffing to shave off a second here, or a tenth of second there, by not having to tie you shoes or something equally crazy in transition, we back packers (racers at the back of the pack) are partying and whooping it up. Every back packer knows that during an Ironman the party begins at the start of the run and ends very late into the night as we cross the line to all of you speedy types applause.

4. Over Training

Now while I have not actually majored in this discipline of race day suckage, I have studied it in depth and I can tell you from firsthand knowledge that this really is one of the worst ways to suck on race day. The reason is obvious, not only have you done way way way too much work before the race, but you get very little of the benefits of under training. For instance athletes that over train tend to blow up (if only in their minds) during a race and never really enjoy the moving back packer party.

Why? Because they never get to the back of the pack.

They tend to miss their race goal by a minute or two, in which case they never make it to the back of the pack. Or worse they think they'll miss their goal by a minute of two and drop out of the race. Believe me when I say that if you intend on using either of these two methods in your next race, it is always much more fun and more enjoyable to under train than to over train.

3. Race Day Blues

A well known professional once told this to a friend of mine, who told it to me who will now pass it along to you:

You know that you always have some good and bad training days, so why do you expect your race days to be any different?

Somehow I tend to think that just because I did all this training, and tapering, and preparing for the race that it will all come together like magic. But just like any training day, race day may dawn when I'm on the wrong side of the bed. In other words, the race could all be a huge train wreck and worse yet it may all be out of my control.

Bad weather, flat tires, equipment failure, accidents, the body's natural rhythm, lack of sleep, and even the common cold have led to terrific feats of race day suckage ... and all of them completely out of my control.

94

Just like training days, race days come in many flavors and some are so sour that you are just bound to suck.

2. Injury

There are two types of triathletes in the world; those who have been injured, and those who will be injured. It is a simple fact of triathlon life that if you train and race long enough, you *will* get injured. It could be something as common as a strain, sprain or blister or something a bit more unusual like pink eye, broken collar bone or broken shoulder.

BTW: Two of my friends are currently out with injuries from different bike accidents suffered while training. One has a broken collar bone and the other has a broken shoulder If your injury is less severe, you'll tend to want to race anyway (race injured). That is the number two way to suck at your next race.

The good news is that unlike overtraining, racing injured gives you a free pass into the back packers club, where the party never ends.

1. Professionalitis

Yes the number one way to really suck at your next race has nothing to do with your body, but everything to do with your mind. It can be summed up in various ways but I like to call it professionalitis. It usually occurs the second or third year into a triathlon race career. It can be triggered by chance meeting with a professional triathlete or an exceptional race results, but the outcome is always the same. Before you know it, you fancy yourself a professional triathlete.

Here are just a few of the warning signs:

You start to dress like a professional triathlete (logos, cool max everything).

95

You have a subscription to both *Inside Tri* and *Triathlete* magazines.

You are a regular and contributing member of slowtwich.com.

You live, eat, and breathe triathlon (Cliff Bars become your favorite treat).

You know all of the Ironman races in North America and are planning on racing every one or HAVE raced every one.

You enter the Kona lottery each year.

You have an Ironman tattoo.

All of your friends are triathletes or endurance athletes.

Your #1 goal in life is to qualify for Kona.

But the biggest warning sign is when racing and training triathlon stops being fun and becomes work. Just like a professional you have now made your passion your job. And by making it into work, you kill your passion. Your entire life begins to revolve around your race performance because after all this is how professionals measure themselves.

More importantly your entire persona starts to depend on how you do at your next race. It is no longer good enough to just finish the race. Instead you need to show, place or better yet win your age group because that's how you qualify for Kona.

But unfortunately the vast majority of us are not talented enough to be professional triathletes, and heaven knows that certainly includes me. We can aspire to compete *like* professionals on race day, but we won't *be* professionals. When we change our expectations to include a personal best at every race, or top ten finish in our age-group, or a Kona slot, we are almost always guaranteed to suck at our next race because we'll never perform up to our own unattainable professional expectations.

So next time you race, **don't forget to savor the race moment**, no matter how fast or slow you go. You worked so very hard (unless, of course, you are like me and have incredible muscle memory) to just get to this point so really enjoy it and HAVE FUN!

When it all goes terribly wrong

The date was June 13, 2004. It was my first half Iron distance race. The race was called the Colorado Triathlon. It is now (thankfully) defunct.

I was about 30 pounds overweight, or as I like to think of myself, right in the prime of the Clydesdale group. I was big-boned in an endurance athlete sort of way. I was packing plenty of self-nutrition. I had my own built in floatation device: my stomach.

I should have known I was heading for trouble earlier in the year. It was just a few weeks before the big race, and I was doing a practice swim in the soon-to-be race lake, when a suspicious object floated by my face.

Normally I don't notice these things but I was a bit edgy as I was swimming in new place with questionable water quality. This object looked vaguely familiar. "Could it be a Snickers?" I thought, but my brain flashed back to that famous scene in Caddy Shack.

Then I looked up and saw that I was swimming by the doggy beach. I should have taken this incident as a sign from God, (Dog spelled backwards). He was telling me to drop out of the race.

Or perhaps I should have dropped out when I learned that the bike course was changed at the last minute. What started out as a pretty reasonable course was shortened to a 10-mile loop that went over the same huge hill ... six times.

I rode up the hill for five miles and down the other side, turned around and did it all over again in the opposite direction. By the third time I had gone up that hill the temperature was well above 90.

My spare tire floatation device was now officially an anchor, and I was already dehydrated just half way into the bike portion of the race. So by the time I rode up that hill three more times, I suspect that I was not thinking straight.

In fact I know I was not thinking straight for I remember dumping out all of my Gatorade before the run, as I actually thought it was too heavy and it might slow me down.

I'm not sure to what extent the race organizers really though through the run course, but they did manage to create an entire half marathon course without a speck of shade. Perhaps they thought it would be good training for Kona, or perhaps they thought that Colorado in June is a dry type of heat so the racers would really enjoy it.

All I remember is that somehow I got it into my head that if I drank two cups of water every mile– and these were the two ounce Dixie cups the dentist gives you to rinse– I would be fine as frog legs.

You see, I thought that I needed **two** cups and not one, since it was so hot. Somehow I neglected to consider that two cups was still only about four ounces. What seemed to really matter to me was that I was doubling my water intake every mile.

And yes; now I understand that two times zero is still pretty much zero. I kept up this strict hydration regime for the first six miles. By mile seven, I was not feeling so well. In fact I was starting to get tunnel vision.

For those of you who have never experience tunnel vision, you're missing out on a real treat. It's just like going to an amusement park except you don't have to wait for the ride. The very ground beneath your feet starts to buckle and sway. You move this way and that, the ground swells up like and ocean waves. In fact you sort of feel like a very nauseous whirling Julia Andrews in the opening scenes from the Sound of Music.

Except in my case the hills were only alive with the sound of about a million bees. It seems that the dirt road, or was it a race course, it was hard to recall, had taken me into the Bee family reunion. And boy was this a big Bee family.

Thousands of Bees buzzed all around me as I swayed with the music. What's worse, I was the only one on the course, as I had been passed by most of the other racers a long time ago.

Somehow I managed to make it through the Bees and found a solitary tree. I sat down under it on the lonely dirt road and contemplated my next more. I was three miles from the finish line and about seven hours into the race at this point. I vaguely recall seeing a medic as he drove by who asked me if I was all right.

The next thing I remember was being in the ambulance with a saline drip in my arm. The world had stopped dancing, and somebody had turned up the air to max. I felt hot and cold at the same time.

My half Iron Distance race was over and I had my first DNF ever. I should have heeded his warning for Dog is my co-pilot. Or is it the other way around?

How big is your endurance engine?

One hundred years ago scientists used to compare the human brain to a clock. Since the clock was one of the most sophisticated pieces of engineering that man had developed at the time, naturally it was compared to a brain.

Today we compare the human brain most often to a computer. Do you think that one hundred years from now people will think that this comparison is ridiculously inadequate, in the same way we look at the clock comparison?

In the year 3006 they might look upon our understanding of the brain with amusement. "Can you really believe that they considered the PC to be as complex as the human brain?" they may say and shake their heads with astonishment.

So what is a good analogy and or comparison to describe the way our bodies work when we race? I'm going to take a stab at this and if you happen to be reading this in the year 3006, feel free to scratch your head and wonder how stupid they were "back-in-the-day."

Over the years I've come to understand that there are three components that make-up a successful triathlete. I'll dare to compare a successful triathlete to a high performance car. (Please chuckle away, Dear Reader from circa 3006).

And just like a fast car the winning triathlete is made up of these three critical components. In order of importance they to you they are:

a) Your Endurance Engine

b) Your Chassis

c) Your Software

Your Endurance Engine

When I first started running I had this notion that I had to run as fast as possible every time I stepped out the front door. My runs would consist of about a half-hour of flogging myself up and down the local street or pushing the speed higher and higher on the treadmill.

Now don't get any crazy notions. I wasn't running five-minute miles. It was more like 12-minute miles, but to me it seemed very fast. It is after all just a matter of perspective.

I also believed that every time I ran, I should also run a bit further in that same half hour. After all my body should be getting fitter and stronger after each run. I didn't realize that I was doing nothing to build up my endurance engine. I was in fact developing my rather poor dragster (sprint) engine when I should have been using my neglected jet (endurance) engine.

A jet engine tends to run best at high speeds for long periods of time.

A dragster engine builds to a lightning fast top speed that takes a car from zero to two hundred in just seconds. However it cannot maintain or even sustain that speed for the time that it takes you to read this sentence. If you keep your foot on the pedal just a little too long ... Kaboom!

So the obvious answer is that you want to be jet powered. You want your endurance engine to be like a powerful jet engine that just goes and goes and goes at the highest possible speed for the longest possible time.

That's the answer, but what's the question? It took me a while to learn the question because the question is really the key to getting fast in this sport.

I'll tell you the question in a second, but first you may want to read your body's owner's manual. I took a look through mine a few years ago and it actually said to use only premium gas(no fast food please), go in for regular check-ups (my doctor is now happy), and don't over-rev the engine if you want it to perform at its peak.

It was then that I realized that the key to going fast for long periods of time was to just go slow. In other words, the best way to build up my endurance jet engine was to train slowly for longer and longer periods of time.

It seems pretty simple but it is damn hard to do. For me it meant keeping my heart rate below 140 when I ran. I have to confess that I want to push myself when I train. I want to feel spent, sore and tired after a workout. Running full out for a half-hour certainly made me feel very tired. But unfortunately it didn't make me much faster at the next race.

But something funny happened when I started running longer at a slower pace while keeping the heart rate below 140. Slowly and over a few months of time I notice that I was running faster and faster miles.

At first I was running 13-minute miles with my heart rate at 140. But over time I noticed that I was able to maintain 12-minute miles and 11 and even 10-minute miles all the while keeping my heart rate at 140.

I also noticed that I wasn't as spent, sore and tired after my long runs. This became a very good thing when I started to take the sport more seriously, and began having a few double workout days during the week.

It may be great to feel spent when you run just a half-hour a few times a week but it really stinks when you still have to bike or swim that same day. It is after all a triathlon, as my coach likes to say.

So what's the question that I finally realized I should have been asking myself?

"How do I increase the power of my endurance engine to run at the highest possible speed for the longest possible time?"

That's the $10,000 dollar question in the sport of triathlon.

The Night Before

The shrill call of the alarm kicks me out of my sound slumber. I've finally fallen asleep and now at four in the morning I stumble out of bed and think to myself, "Exactly why the heck am I doing this?"

It's always the same for me no matter what the race. It can be a marathon, a triathlon, or century ride, but when 4 a.m. eventually rolls around and I'm stumbling through some strange hotel room, in the coldest part of the morning, I start to seriously question why I don't just take up golf.

Imaging being able to roll up to the country club at 10 a.m. and have a helpful and courteous man takes your clubs to an electric golf cart that comes complete with 800 beer holders.

All you have to do is ride up to the first tee, gently swing a club, and wait for the beer girl to bring by the libation, and perhaps a Snickers bar for the long ride up the first fairway.

Instead I've just stubbed my toe on the hard corner of the gloomy bed while I dig around in my bag in the semi-dark for my race number belt.

It's always like this no matter what the race. The night before is always the worst. To start with we go to some restaurant that promises all you can eat pasta.

Why pasta?

Because sometime just before the First World War, and during the ice age of running somebody decided that pasta was the official pre-race food.

Why?

Because it is a well known fact that Philippides (the messenger sent from the plain of marathon to Sparta for help, and even though he was Greek), just loved pasta. He loved it so much that during his famous 150-mile run he stopped at every pizza joint along the way and ordered a triple helping of the stuff.

Sadly his legacy remains, so today we must all strap on the pasta feedbag before every race. Not only does it make us feel like we're Olympic athletes, but here in Boulder (where we have lots of races) it accounts for 50 percent of the Olive Garden's net profits.

By far the worst part of the pre-race dinner is that we can't have any alcohol, and boy do I need it. I'm already nervous. Not because I know I'm just hours away from my A race, but because I know I'm about to try something that very few athletes in the world have ever accomplished. That would be to fall asleep early on a race night.

I dutifully head back to the hotel room at like 7 p.m. and jump in bed. Six hours later I'm still awake having watched four hours of CNN and the weather channel. I've also managed to try to fall asleep in every sleep position known to mankind, and that includes the way the ancient Egyptians used to sleep with a curved wooden dowel under their necks. No kidding ... Google it.

I've been to the bathroom a total of 9,585 times since I drank 9,585 glasses of water at dinner. And I've manages to tangle myself up in those freakin' hotel room bed sheets in such a way that Houdini would not be able to escape the vise-like grasp of the bed.

So if you do the math, and believe me I have not, that means that I fell into a deep slumber at about 3.35 a.m., which means I have a grand total of 25 minutes of sleep before the alarm wakes me up.

And now it is time to again try something that very few, if any, athletes have ever managed to do. And no I'm not talking about an Ironman. An Ironman is a piece of cake compared to the torture of trying to make yourself go to the bathroom when you don't have to. And just to be very clear here I'm talking about number two.

Because if you don't go now, you know that the second the race starts your bowels will defiantly try to explode.

I remember the start of this year's Moab half marathon. The race starts well up a canyon with only about 50 port-a-potties at the start. Now, 50 may seem like a lot but not when compared to thousand racers with defiant bowls.

The race start resembles a huge life-sized-bang-a-mole game. The bang-a-mole game is a kid's Chucky Cheese favorite. These little moles pop out of their holes and the crazed kids bang them with a giant mallet.

It's the same way at the start of the Moab half marathon. Dozens of racers at the start are squatting behind boulders and bushes with only the tops of their sweaty heads poking out. Their red face and beady little eyes taunt you mercilessly. If I only had a giant mallet and a bunch or quarters!

It is this type of thinking that spurs me to do my duty in the hotel but alas, as I'm sure you must know, this is a fool's mission. The body will of course wait until the start of the race, which happens to perfectly coincide with the time we normally wake up.

Exiting the bathroom I am left with one main task … the pre-race breakfast. After years of racing I now know exactly what I should and must eat before a big race.

It is tempting to switch my routine to something from the hotel's breakfast room, so I do. It's funny how the temptation of a free muffin and coffee can potentially ruin an entire race that I've trained for over the past year.

Perhaps it is because I'm not thinking too clearly after just 25 minutes of sleep. Or perhaps it is because I'm an age-group racer and perhaps a muffin and coffee are just what I need to get me through the race.

Does your Zip determine your Zip?

What factors do you believe will be most influential on how you perform at your next race? Is it your fitness level, or perhaps the amount of training you did before the race, or could it be your nutrition, or perhaps it's your equipment, or is it just plain luck?

A recent study we just compiled here at Everyman Triathlon has found a surprising answer to this question. We followed 5,000 triathlete nurses for over five years. We painstakingly compiled not only their race results, but also their daily diet, their workout regime, their family histories, their lottery and Vegas winnings, and we logged their complete clothing and equipment preferences, along with everything else we learned into a massive database.

We took these results and compared them to a double-blind study of an additional 5,000 triathlete nurses and tabulated the results to once and for all settle the question of what is the most influential factor in race day performance. The results are both shocking and enlightening.

Lessons Learned

So for just five easy payment of $99.95 we'll send you the results of this groundbreaking study. Plus if you act today we'll also include our patented Butt Burn Weasel. The Butt Burn Weasel is a revolutionary new device that we developed at the Everyman Tri Laboratories over a period of 12 long years.

The BB Weasel is guaranteed to sooth and comfort your raw and tender butt checks after a long ride with its patented messaging paws. Just clamp it on to any 4-inch or thicker belt, bend over the kitchen table, and let the BB Weasel message away those miles with a patented circular rubbing and thumping motion. Act today as supplies are limited!

You know I'm just kidding.

But it does make you think as to what one factor influence how you'll do at your next race. I've been thinking about this a lot recently and I've come to a surprising conclusion. I suspect that where you live has a lot to do with how you will perform at your next race.

I believe this in part because I've been reading a lot of Blogs and I'm always surprised at how bad the weather is many parts of this country and world. I'm amazed that many triathletes can train at all during the winter.

The training reports are filled with cold, wet, snowy, windy, icy, and in general crappy weather. I find it hard enough to go out for my daily workout when the weather is sunny and warm, I'm truly amazed that you can do it when a Tornado is heading down your street, and yet somehow you do.

A few years ago I ran the Las Vegas marathon. In my build-up to the race I ended up having to do my long run (20 miles) on the treadmill because it was icy outside and I didn't want to risk falling and hurting myself.

The first hour of this treadmill run was uneventful. The second hour I started to get really bored and I found myself looking for anything to relieve the boredom like trying to anticipate when the little red light on the treadmill would jump one point ahead. By hour three I was ready to stick a very pointy screwdriver into my ear. I was both completely bored and completely exhausted. This is not an easy combination to achieve.

There are even bigger factors (beside the weather) that make it easier for us living in Boulder to train. For instance when I look out my window I see people running and biking all the time. You can't swing a dead Butt Burn Weasel in Boulder without hitting somebody on a bike or a run.

In fact it seems downright strange to live here and not be training for something. Not only is this town full of professional triathletes, but we have Olympic runners and cyclist and even our fair share of professional adventure racers.

Last year I happened to go on a ride with this group of pro athletes and I have to admit that they make Ironman triathletes look like weekend coach potatoes. Forget this sissy stuff like riding your rode bike for a "short" 80-mile loop. This is not good enough for these adventure racer types.

We get about five miles into the ride and they say let's take the back roads. So we find the nearest dirt road, they let some air out of their tires, and away we go for a 80-mile adventure ride. By about mile 20, I'm shaken and certainly well stirred as I'm on my ultra-stiff aluminum road bile. By mile, 30 my legs, lungs and front derailleur have gone south. By mile 40, I can barely keep up and my front brake is broke. At mile 45 I bail out of the ride, but they keep going, as now they are finally warmed-up.

When you live in a place full of these types of athletes, it is almost expected that you spend Saturday morning going long. Two weeks ago in Chicago, I went for a nice nine-mile run. I had to drive about a half hour just to get to a forest preserve so I could run on trail, instead of on the street or sidewalk.

Here in Boulder I have about four dozen trails to choose from within a 10-minute drive of my house. But many people might just as easily ride their bikes to the trail or on the trail. Almost every road in town has a bike lane. I'd be terrified to bike in most U.S cities on the road.

Finally, I'm amazed at how committed you must be to swim on a regular basis in many places around the country. I know I take this for granted but we have four recreation centers that each other numerous Masters classes per day, plus two health clubs that have their own Masters classes every day...one of which is taught by six-time Ironman world champion Dave Scott.

We here at Everyman triathlon salute all of you have athletes who have to plan, drive, scrape, and struggle and just to work out. You are the ones who really deserve that free Butt Burn Weasel. So act today, as supplies are definitely limited.

Transition Dos and Don'ts

Raise your hand if you can tell me the best place to rack your bike in the transition area.

Anybody?

If you said nearest to the bike exit you are get today's gold star award.

So now for the tougher question, why do you want to be near the bike exit and not near the run exit, or by yourself in a remote corner of transition, or near the swim entrance, or at home sleeping in and eating a glazed chocolate covered donut for breakfast?

Never mind that last part of that question as I don't have a good answer to "Donut Conundrum" as I like to call it. Why am I up at this predawn God forsaken hour racking my bike anyway always comes to mind ... all too often as I'm stumbling in the dark getting ready for yet another bout of triathlon torture.

Anyway, conventional transition wisdom, at least as taught to me by the local Boulder professional tri Zen masters, states that the closer you are to the bike exit in transition the less distance you have to cover (both going out and coming in to transition) while:

a) Pushing your bike though a maze of racks
b) Running in bike shoes (never fun or fast)

110

c) Running in bare feet if you happen to have your bike shoes attached to your bike

So now that we have the optimal location of your bike sorted, here are some other transition do's and don'ts:

Do get to transition early to stake out the idea spot for your gear.

Don't stumble into transition one minute before it is scheduled to close and expect to have a good race as you try to rack your bike, put on sun screen, sort out your shoes, sun glasses and race number and go to the bathroom (both #1 and #2) all at the same time.

Do be polite and friendly to your fellow racers and happily share your sunscreen, and/or any other necessary triathlon commodity that they may have forgot and you have in spades.

Why?

Because you can bet that what comes around goes around. That person who just borrowed your sunscreen will certainly be the one who will have that extra tube that you realized you forgot when you flat on the bike course.

Don't be the one in transition who is so into their race plan that the slightest smile or comment from a fellow racer sends them into a dizzy of anger and/or an emotional hissy fit. Unless your last name happens to be Woods, Jordan, Schumacher, or Armstrong you probably haven't had the results and earned the right to be or act like a prima donna.

Do place your bike and gear in any kind of order that works best for you. I like to put down a towel next to my bike. On the towel I place the following items from front to back with back being closets to the rack:

Front row: Triathlon bike shoes with or without socks lying on top of them. Olympic distance or less I go sockless. I also love my tri bike shoes, as the Velcro strap is designed to stay open with little notches just for this purpose.

Back row: Running shoes with race number attached to race belt stuffed in one shoe with running hat on top of shoes.

I like to have my bike helmet upside down on my areo bars and my sunglasses in the helmet. This way when running from the swim I first put on the sun glasses, followed by the helmet, followed by the bike shoes. The helmet first rule ensures that I don't forget this critical part of the swim to bike transition as not having a helmet on the bike qualifies for an immediate DQ during most races.

Don't touch other racers' bike or stuff. This seems self-evident, but all too often I see this #1 rule being broken all the time. I (like you) have my stuff just the way I want it, and need it, so please don't mess with it.

Do try to hang your bike by the rear seat so that it faces out (front wheel forward). This is a great technique that makes it super fast and easy to just

grab your bike and go. All you have to do is hang your bike by the front of the seat from the rack. In other words, just place the pole of the rack under the front of your bike seat (see photo above).

Don't hang your bike by the brake levers from the pole. I have seen racers get their bikes stuck on their brakes and almost take down the entire rack trying to wrestle it free.

Do zero out your bike odometer/computer before the start of the race.

Don't clear your computer: when you are leaving transition, while clipping into your pedals, while climbing up a hill, or while trying to avoid the rest of us and most likely crashing in a pile of sweat and shame.

Do get a transition bag. I have a huge and terrific backpack transition bag from Zipp that holds everything including my pet elephant. This makes life so much easier before and after the race that I can't believe I ever raced without it.

Don't try to bring all of your stuff into transition in your everyday gym bag while riding or pushing your bike. Chances are it won't fit and you'll crash juggling your bike

and gear to transition in a heap of sleepy-eyed slumber and shame.

Do transition quickly and efficiently so that you spend your time racing.

Don't spend a lot of time in transition during the race because transitions really do count and you can make up huge amounts of time just by getting in and out fast. I'm hope you believe me when I say that it is a lot easier to make up three minutes in transition as opposed to on the run. If you don't believe me just try to drop a minute a mile on your next sprint tri three mile run and see how easy that is to accomplish.

Don't blow dry your hair in transition!

This weekend I raced a small local triathlon that claims to be—and probably is— Colorado's oldest race. In the past, the racers ran from the pool swim, through the recreation center locker rooms to the transition area in the parking lot. A friend of mine mentioned to me that when she first did this triathlon (her first) she stopped in the ladies locker room and blow-dried her hair before heading out to the bike.

This certainly qualifies as one of the top don'ts for any race situation.

And finally, for goodness sake: **Don't forget your towel!**

Chapter 6

Race Reports

The Las Vegas Marathon

The wind slapped me hard, like the quick hand of a Victorian father against the rosy cheeks of his misbehaving, capricious 10-year-old child.

They say the number 13 is unlucky and it certainly was for me. Up until the halfway point of the marathon everything was going great. The weather was great, I felt great, and I was well within my half way goal pace of two hours.

The terrific thing about the old Las Vegas marathon course is that is was completely unimaginative. At the crack of down, they would drive you out of town down the highway for 26 miles, like some unwanted outlaws, and you got to run back to town in a straight line along the highway on the frontage road. Your crime, of course, was being way too fit for a city that thrives on booze and cigarettes.

I remember walking to the buses through the MGM Grand Casino at 5 on a Sunday morning. It was packed with dull-eyed, chain smoking, slot machine feeding, whisky drinking gamblers who I'm sure didn't just get up to go for a quickie bet. These folks had been at it all night, but since there is no night in a casino, it could have been the middle of the afternoon as far as they knew.

I've always had a sort of warped view of power and freedom. To me true power and freedom represent the power and freedom **not** to do something, versus the more traditional view that power and freedom allows you to do, or be, or accomplish something.

Here's what I mean. Do you think that Bill Gates carries a cell phone, or does he have people that carry his cell phone? I know that I would love to chuck my cell phone out of the window. It represents an albatross around my neck that keeps me tethered to work 24/7.

OK, so that's a pretty silly example, but here's another one I hope illustrates my meaning better. When I looked around the casino at 5 a.m. I didn't see a lot of people having fun. In fact you rarely see what I would consider an expression of fun and joy on a gambler's face. They tend to look more like people at work. They seems really intent on what they are doing in a sort of "don't bother me, I'm too busy right now" way that folks get on deadline.

So the question in my mind has always been are these folks truly free? Do they really want to be gambling at 5 on a Sunday morning? I suppose they could have asked the same question of me. Did I really want to be up at 5 a.m. for a cold ride into the gloomy dessert only to have to run back to town for 26.2 miles into a howling headwind?

Actually it was only the last 13 miles that the wind got really nasty. And by nasty I mean that it was so strong that we knew when we were close to a water station before we could actually see the damn thing by the legions of empty tumbling cups that hit our feet as we ran.

And by we, I mean the bike-like draft line that about 10 of us formed to try to beat the wind. Just like a bike team time trial, we would take turns at the front of the group.

As I was both the tallest and widest, I seemed to get much more encouragement to stay at the front of the line. The 5-foot 4-inch girl who was ahead of me did a great job in shielding my stomach against the wind, but that was about all. And since my stomach already has a somewhat rounded aerodynamic shape, I'm not sure what good she really did. All I remember is thinking how grateful I was that all of my energy was spent on the wind and not on the course.

I ran a different marathon a few years ago in Logan, Utah where the last part of the race coiled through town like a drunken snake. All I recall was how mentally tough every turn was as the race neared the finish. I didn't mind running that last six miles, but it was all those crazy turns that made the last part a stumbling death march.

Which brings me back to power– or lack of it!

I've really come to believe that if you have done the work, your success or failure in any race hinges not on your strength, or fitness, or stamina, but on your mental power. To what extent can you push your mind over whatever is the matter with your body or the conditions, or your luck?

Because there will always be something that will limit your performance.

In Las Vegas, it was the wind. In Utah, it was the crazy winding course at the end of the marathon. The biggest difference between the two races for me was my brainpower.

In Vegas, I pushed myself through the wind to a personal best marathon time of just over four hours. In Logan, I folded like a cheap deck of cards. My body was ready for both races but I lacked the brainpower in Logan to get the job done.

Post   Script:
The craziest thing about the Las Vegas marathon was that both my neighbor and I had the exact same time....to the hundredth decimal place. Yes we

trained together and roomed together, but there is no way in this world that we could ever replicate that finish time again. I bet that if we tried to run together and cross the finishing mat at the same time (a hundredth of a second is just such a half blink of time) that we could never replicate our identical times.

I cracked like a Walnut: Disney Half Ironman

Just seconds prior to the start of the Disney race I heard a guy next to me say that he was just hoping to finish. He said that he signed up for the race but that life got in the way of his training.

I wish I could blame my lack of training on my results, but I did train.

I wish I could blame a broken collarbone, but I was break free.

I wish I could blame a mechanical mishap, but the only thing that really went wrong was I broke my sunglasses before the bike, and that's no real reason to really slow down.

I wish I could blame my cabin mates on a long night of partying or even excessive snoring, but they were great.

As my friend Bolder likes to say, I cracked like a walnut on the run.

The only consolation I had was sitting at the finish eating my pizza and listening to the race announcer. As the time ticked well into the seven hour pace he kept repeating. "and here comes another big guy crossing the line with a strong finish."

The fact is that we Clydesdales don't tend to do well in the heat. And the hotter it gets, the worse we do. We are just too big and carrying too much weight to perform well when the temperature rises into the mid-to-high nineties.

The funny thing is that I don't really consider myself all that big. I currently weigh 218 pounds, but I really think of myself as a small-ish guy in an over sized world.

"If they allowed drafting in this race, I'd be tucked in behind you," a small guy said as he passed me on his bike.

It's not until people actually mention something to me, like the guy on the bike, that I realize that I'm all that big.

But I certainly felt every ounce of my 218 Clydesdale poundage on the run. I started out strong for about the first half mile, to the cheers of the run exit crowd. I was well within cracking a personal best time. All I had to do was run a sub 2:15 half marathon. This should not be a problem for me. Just a few months ago I ran a 1:55 half in Moab.

The general rule of thumb is to expect to go about ten percent slower on a triathlon run than your normal run time for any given distance.

So theoretically a sub 2:15 half marathon time was well within my reach. My best half IM to date has been a 5:55 so I knew I could crack it, but the course and sun had other plans.

All too quickly the three loop run at Disney became a survival shuffle through Death Valley.

The run took a left from the pavement for a donkey path along a dirty, dusty, hot, sweaty and snaky canal path for the next three miles.

And by snaky I don't mean that it twisted around like a snake. No it was perfectly straight. But I do mean that black angry looking five-foot python that slithered just across the path in front of my causing me to slam on the brakes. Now keep in mind that my brakes (read calve muscles) were pretty gone at this point, so the sudden stop caused them to seize like a bad brake job from your local Brakes-R-Us hut.

My heart rate jumped, the gal in the death march behind me slammed into my back, and I began jumping up and down like I had just crashed a fire ant party in bare feet.

That was the official beginning of the end. Whatever iota of will that had remained in my body departed, and I was officially toast. For the rest of the run, I just wanted to be done and back in the cool, air-conditioned comfort of my Disney cabin, complete with little hand towels done up like Disney characters

The one true feeling that I was left to contemplate for the next 12 miles was that Disney really didn't want this race on their property. They sort of grudgingly allowed it, as it brings in about 5,000 people, but they certainly don't want the racers stinking up their park.

Case and point: This is the third year of the race. The first year it was a one-loop run. The second year they shortened it to a two-loop run which included a short death march on this snaky, sun-baked, uneven, shadeless and shameless unused donkey trail. This year almost 70 percent of the run was an out and back on this dusty donkey trial. I suspect next year Disney will make sure that no runners stink up their shady well-maintained, paved walking and running trials by making the entire run in the swampy canal instead of the swampy canal path.

Ironman will call it the Disney swap challenge and racers will be given the choice to either run or swim the last leg of the race.

Some of you may believe that I'm exaggerating a bit. You are wrong.

The only part of my leg that was even a bit whitish after the race was formed by the strap that held my chip in place. From my ankles to just below knees, my legs looked I had just waded through a bucket of dirty black paint. My shoes, as well as those of my cabin mates, were so filthy dirty that they are now officially only good for lawn mowing duty.

It looks like I'll be purchasing a new set of racing shoes. Not that this pair was all that fast. I finished the half marathon in just under 2:45. That would be a survival shuffle with long walks through the water stations.

My overall time was just over 6:20. This was much better than last year but for next year I would personally rename the race to the Disney Nutcracker.

Post note: Funniest thing I saw all day was a guy about 20 feet ahead of me on the bike trying to negotiate the very tight turnaround on the second out and back portion of the bike course.

He had a disk wheel so he really had to slow down to make the sharp U-turn. He kept going slower and slower and slower until he came to a complete stop, and plopped over like a fresh cut tree. TIM - BER!

Dude, I'm sorry I know that must have really hurt, as you looked like you were still clipped in, but it sure looked funny.

Chicago Triathlon---Big Bumblebee Guy

I immediately noticed that the big bumblebee guy ahead of me had a 37 on his calf. At the Chicago triathlon, the world's largest triathlon with over eight thousand athletes, they start the race in waves. They put all of the direct competitors into these waves, and instead of writing your age on your calf, they brandish your calve with your wave number.

So when I noticed that the big bumblebee guy just ahead of me had a 37 on his calf, just like me, I knew the race was on.

I decided to call him the big bumblebee guy because:

1) He was big like me.
2) He wore a bright yellow and black race suit.
3) He had flown by me like an angry bee on the bike.

Now we were on the run just about a mile from the finish. For those of you who have never raced the Chicago Triathlon the word "big" best describes the race. At any given time you are completely surrounded by hundreds of other athletes. It is not uncommon to ride four or five abreast on the bike section. The run resembles that of a big city marathon, with a huge snaking procession of athletes pounding the pavement.

It is very rare indeed to be able to pick out your direct competition.

Now, theoretically, we're all competing for the fastest overall course time, but in reality as an age-group triathlete you're more likely racing the clock and yourself for a personal best. Or even more likely you just want to finish the race running. Or even more likely, especially if you are a newbie, you just want to finish the race.

So it was something completely new and unexpected for me when I found myself on the run actually racing another athlete. Over the years and over the dozens of triathlons I've never actually raced another athlete head to head. I'm usually by myself trying to finish the race before it gets dark ... like at my last Ironman. Or I'm racing, but because of the way the race is structured, I am never certain if the other athletes around me are in my age group. This means that they could or could not be competing with me.

With this uncertainty, I tend to ignore the potential competition and focus on my stopwatch as a way to motivate myself. I think that's the way most of us age-groupers race.

So here I was at mile 5 and just minutes before the finish line of the world's largest triathlon with the big bumblebee guy, my direct competition, dead ahead of me. In a single heartbeat the stopwatch became meaningless and it was Game On!

I had of course seen this type of race situation a hundred times before on television. You know when two triathletes or marathon runners are coming to the end of a really close and thrilling race and they are running inches in front of each other.

It was just like that for me now. I was just behind the big bumblebee guy and we racing for the podium position. Of course I didn't that this race was for an age group podium position, which it turned out it was, but I knew my time was fast and that time it really counted.

So of course I made my first mistake. I passed the big bumblebee guy running up a small hill. Now many of you may be picturing the dramatic end of a very close ITU race were the triathletes all but dive across the finish line to win the race. Or perhaps you are imaging the Boston Marathon were the elite runner's surge from a 5:00 minute mile pace to a 4:30 to test each other's strength and resolve.

No no no, this was not my move. You would be completely wrong. I suspect if you had been watching this race from your house and we had come running by it would have looked like two chunky neighbors out for a Sunday jog with one passing the other in a sort of slow motion painful spurt of energy.

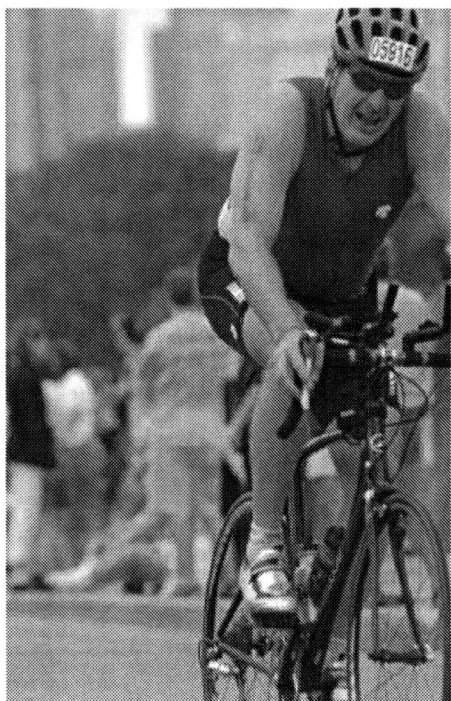

And of course my mistake was that I did this going up a hill. Because the second I passed him he of course noticed the big black 37 on my calf. What happened? He immediately sped up and passed me just as the hill flattened out. You must realize that when two big boys race up a hill at the end of an Olympic distance race nobody is going to zip or indeed surge ahead.

And so it was now, we were winding our way through the last mile of the course with him having upped the tempo to perhaps a blinding fast 9:40 mile pace. Just to put this in perspective for you, a professional Kenyan or Ethiopian runner cannot actually run so painfully slowly, or indeed match our pace until they are well over the age of 95.

But here we were locked in our own slow motion battle. It was exact at this moment that all of my sitting on couch and watching television paid off. Perhaps if he had spent more time in front of the TV he would have won this day.

I recalled the invisible string that attaches runners racing at the same pace. Or at least I recalled the television commentators talking about this invisible string. All I had to do was to break the string that bound us together.

Lucky for me the racecourse took a slight downward direction. On the small uphill to the transition area I kicked in the afterburners and blew by him at perhaps a stupendously dizzying 9:10 pace, and never looked back.

"Never ever looked back," the television commentators always say. "This is a sign of weakness and defeat."

So I sprinted to the end using the powerful pull of a hearty lunch to get me across the finish line ahead of the big bumblebee guy. In fact the call of a good Chinese lunch was so strong that I didn't stick around for the awards ceremony.

It wasn't until I got back home to Colorado that a friend of mine said they had called out my name at the awards ceremony. I had taken second place in my age group and more importantly…I apparently cracked the big bumblebee guy like a walnut.

It just goes to show the power of television and good Chinese takeout !

My First Triple Bypass

It all happened in slow motion so it seemed completely unreal. Unfortunately the embarrassment that soon followed was all too real.

I was climbing as well as a 220 pound guy can climb up a steep mountain pass about 60 miles into Colorado's infamous Triple Bypass yearly bike ride.

I still had another 60 miles to go to complete the ascent and descent of three very long and steep mountain passes to get to the finish line in Avon, Colorado. I reached into my back pocket to get a gel when I lost concentration and dropped with a thud from the road like an over ripe apple onto the loose sand they were using to pad the new tarmac.

One second I was climbing and the next I was lying on the side of the road like beached whale still clipped into my pedals. About every two seconds a rider would yell out, "Are you OK?," as I struggled to free my bound feet.

I was totally fine except for the fact that I couldn't get free from my shackle-like clips. I had just taken the world's slowest fall into the world's softest sand. It was like plopping into fresh powder, except warmer and much more embarrassing.

After struggling for about five minutes like an unturned turtle, I figured out it was easier just to slip out of my shoes and be done with it.

Standing only in my socks by the side of the road I was happy to have restored what little dignity I still had left as I got back on my road bike for the rest of this crazy adventure.

When I first moved to Colorado I had of course heard about the Triple Bypass. It was a legendary ride for a few crazy types who were willing to try to ride just over 120 miles with three mountain passes and over 10,000 feet of elevation gain. Just to put it into perspective, that's about an average day in the Alps for the boys on the Tour de France.

And please note that I don't —and indeed have never— shaved my legs. That's about the level of rider I am when compared to a serious cyclist.

I knew I was in for a long hard day when I started the ride at 6:30 a.m. with a nice steep two-hour warm-up climb to the top of the first pass. There was no dinner, no foreplay, no pleasant conversation ... just a sharp right turn after I mounted my bike and right into the granny gear. In fact, I have never before in my life spent so much time in such a teeny tiny gear.

As much as I love my BMC Time Machine, this was no time to for bravery so I wisely opted to ride my Giant road bike with a triple gear for the Triple Bypass. I did see one guy (from Manchester, England as it turned out) on a triathlon Scott time trial bike, but he was not nearly as amused as I was by his valiant struggle up the mountains.

I reached the top of the first pass at 8:30 a.m. feeling pretty proud and smug. I had now covered about the first 12 miles of the ride in just under two hours. When I did the math my heart sank, I was averaging just about six miles-an-hour. Let's keep this perspective train rolling. The boys on the tour climbed two very similar mountains in the Alps today and the leaders averaged about 39-kilometers an hour ... which is about 1 million more miles an hour than I could ever dream about.

Well there was nothing I could do about it but fill up my empty water bottles and begin the long descent to Idaho Springs. That part was easy. Now I'm sure that no one would ever mistake me for a contender for the "King of the Mountains" polka dot jersey. I'm not small, I'm not thin, I'm certainly not Columbian and I'm certainly not dancing on my bike as I struggle up even the smallest grade.

I can, however descend like the wind. All that weight and bulk that are such a huge anchor on the climb magically turn into a powerful booster rocket on the descent. Usually very few cyclists can pass me on a downhill unless I sit up and let them. So naturally I really love this part of the mountain rides. Unfortunately, in the mountains, what goes down has to go up. All too soon I was climbing again and this time up I-70 toward Loveland Pass.

This is by far the worst stretch of the Triple Bypass as all two thousand riders must negotiate about a five-mile stretch of the highway just before the Loveland ski area. And this part of the ride is not only dangerous, as cars whiz by at over seventy miles an hour, but also smelly and dirty, as huge semi-trailer trucks and overloaded RVs struggle up toward the Eisenhower Tunnel spewing huge clouds of spent diesel fuel.

It came as a great relief when I saw the exit toward Loveland Pass, because I knew the highway would soon be behind me, and the lunch stop lay just minutes ahead.

Lunch was fast pb-and-j and J sandwich followed by a few slices of watermelon. I really wish the organizers of such epic rides took the lead from Ironman and provided some Coke or Pepsi at these rest stops. For me nothing tops the tank up on a huge effort quite like a bit of cold sugar water with massive amounts of caffeine.

I stopped drinking soda a few years ago because it really is a huge and needless sugar bomb when combined with a typical lunch or dinner, but during an Ironman or Epic ride a huge sugar bomb fortified with caffeine is just what my body craves.

Instead I filled up my water bottle with water and plopped in a Nuun tablet. When I was first sponsored by Nuun I wasn't really sure how my body would react to the new stuff, but over the last several months I have really come to appreciate the ease and convenience of the little tablets. Unlike the mystery aide drink they had on the ride, the Nuun is always the right consistency and taste. When they mix up the power drinks at the rest stop they always seem to use different amounts of powder and this means that sometimes it taste just right but most times it is either too strong or too week.

I actually used up an entire bottle of Nuun tablets on the ride, and I was so happy to have such a convenient and personal supply of my very own perfect hydration mix.

After recovering from my fall, I met up with some of the other brave raceAthletes at the top of Loveland Pass. It was so nice to see a few friendly faces among the sea of strangers. That's really one of the greatest parts of team raceAthlete … the ability to show up at a race or a ride and know that you have somebody to share your pain and/or joy.

I was now just over halfway through the ride. In fact I had finished the hardest part of the ride. What I didn't know was that the Triple Bypass would throw me a bit of curve.

Why do they call it the Triple Bypass?

That's what I kept wondering as I flew down the back side of Loveland Pass.

There really is no feeling like descending fast on a bike after a huge climb. You really feel like you've just sprouted wings. After hours of slogging it up hill at some ridiculously tedious and painfully slow pace (in fact, I do believe a very energetic inchworm passed me as I plodded up the pass), the descent feels like you are an immediate contender to win the Tour de France.

As I was flying down the hill, a small voice in the back of my mind kept screaming, "Slow down."

Almost 10 years ago I had ridden this very descent for the first time on a mountain bike that was retrofitted with street tires. It was my first taste of mountain riding. I just climbed the hardest pass of my life, so I was jubilantly flying down the hill, tucked into a very precarious and very silly aero position on a bike that was not designed for fast descents.

Just before a very dangerous and steep curve, I heard a sound that at first meant nothing to me, but today would scare the hell out of me. It was loud pop or ping … almost a muffled shot gun blast. I was descending at about 45-miles-an-hour, heading toward a curve with a thousand-foot drop just past a stubby guard rail.

My bike started to buck and bob like a crazed bull with a hornet in its ear. The back end of the bike wobbled so furiously that my vision blurred. I clamped on the brakes, but the rear one merely pulsated as it caught and released. As I hurtled straight for the abyss just inches past the guardrail, my front brake caught.

The only thing that saved my life that day (for I was heading straight for the guardrail and there was no doubt in my mind that I would catapult over it and into the valley thousands of feet below) was the fact that the spoke that popped was on my back wheel. If you have ever had a spoke break you'll know that in an instant the wheel goes out of true. This is usually a minor problem, but when you are flying down a mountain on a mountain bike with well over two hundred pounds on it, the wheel can easily pancake. This recently happened to a friend of mine who did not walk away from the fall.

But back to today. As I now flew down the very same road, this frightening scenario kept replaying in my head over and over again. By the third showing I was on my brakes. I suspect that it is the ability to ignore that little screaming voice in the back of your head that creates some of the greatest cyclist in the world.

This Tour wannabe was all over the brakes. I had nothing to prove and two significant mountain passes still looming in my future.

They officially call it Swan Mountain Pass on the road sign but for some reason the organizers of the Triple Bypass have completely ignored it in their marketing. It comes between Loveland Pass and Vail Pass, but you'll hear no mention of it in the official tile of the ride as in Quadruple Bypass.

Why not?

I suspect that it would be the straw that would break the camels back for many riders when signing up for the ride. "Sure honey, I think I can do three mountain passes and 120 miles in the saddle," the conversation might go. But four mountain passes, well that's just one too many.

And that's exactly how I was feeling climbing up Swan Mountain Pass. I was ready for Vail Pass, but instead I had to climb this bonus pass. Which would normally not be a big deal, but when you are blown, cracked, exploded like a walnut dropped on a busy truck-clogged interstate, even a small hill is a problem. A small mountain pass might as well be the summit of Everest.

There comes a point for us hairy-legged Everymen (and I suspected even shaved-legged Everywoman) in any long ride when the legs explode. The symptoms are simple and straightforward. One of the large muscle groups in the legs cramps up to the point of immobility. Oh yes ... and it hurts like hell.

The muscles just cramp up and stubbornly refuse to move. They let you know they mean business by sending waves of painful stabbing agony to your brain when you try to so much as unlock or twitch the seized up muscle group.

This happened to the muscles on the inside of my thighs on the way up Loveland Pass. Funny thing that; I didn't even know that I had muscles on the inside of my thighs.

Now these same muscles were just screaming at me again saying if I even so much as try to put down any serious power they would go on strike and stand at rigid attention until I got into the nearest sag wagon.
So it was only with kind and very gentle persuasion that I was able to coax them up and over Swan Mountain Pass. By the time I got to the second to last rest stop at the bottom of the pass I was ready to call it a day. But in for a dime, in for a dollar, as I like to say. So I got back on the bike and headed out.

Needless to say, by this point (some 85AAAAHHHHH!!!!!miles and eight hours into the ride) my ass was on fire and I was running on pure stubborn determination. I had my head down and I was now on this death ride to the very end. You know when you get into that mental zone when nothing matters but the finish. In fact I was so into the zone that a car crash on the road next to me didn't even garner my attention. I heard the skid followed by the sound of crunching plastic and metal and looked up as two cars collided in a nasty fender bender.

I just put my head down and kept pedaling. There were tons of police all around and besides the only thing I could have done at that moment was to stop, and tumble from the bike like a newly cut tree, and hope that someone would stand me back up, while I tried not to add to the carnage.

With the accident behind me I now had about a 15 mile climb to the top of the last pass. Vail Pass loomed in my future like Moby Dick...huge, frightening and unconcerned.

I began the ascent in earnest at Copper Mountain. I had climbed this pass from the Copper side many times. It usually takes about a half hour and makes for a very pleasant ride next to a babbling stream. Happy-go-lucky vacationers stroll up and down the pass taking in the massive mountain vistas while breathing in the hundreds of intoxicating wild flower fragrances.

I didn't see any of this. All I saw was the cement path about three feet in front of me. I begged, pleaded, and exhorted my thigh muscles to just keep clicking over. I was now in the home stretch of the death ride and all I had to do was make it to the aid station at the top of the pass. Mercifully the organizers had put the last aid station about twenty miles from Avon. The rest of the ride was all downhill from that aid station at the top of Vail Pass.

All I had to do was make it to the top of the pass and I could coast to the finish. I knew from prior experience that the last quarter mile of the path kicks up viciously and no matter how much I wished it were not so, the path had indeed not changed. About an eighth of a mile from the summit the pass took an especially nasty left turn skyward and my legs called it quits.

That was it they said and cramped up solid like titanium. I just stood there mortified straddling my bike and watched the other riders crest the hill and stop at the aid station. I didn't know what to do. There was no way I could get back on my bike, clip in, and continue up the hill. So I did the only thing left to me. I dismounted and goose stepped up the hill like a Nazi marching on parade before WWII dragging my bike behind me. I was embarrassed, but

I was not able to bend my knees…but I was also not defeated.

When the road evened out a bit I was able to get back on the bike and climb the last few hundred feet the aid station which was just one parking lot level from the tippy top of Vail Pass.

I took on some more water and waited for the rest of the raceAthlete gang to join me. The had waited a bit longer at the previous rest stop to group up while I had gone ahead knowing they would catch me.

When they did we rode as a group to the very top of Vail Pass. This is where I almost puked. The tiny amount of effort to just ride that last little bit was a climb to far. My body was spent and I knew it. I felt like I had just completed and Ironman and now I was feeling weak, sick and all I wanted to do was lay down under a shady tree.

And this is exactly what I did when I finally coasted to the finish in Avon. Actually, I first loaded up my plate with chicken and a burger at the after ride feed. Unfortunately while my mind thought I was hungry my body refused to eat. I took a bite of the burger and a bite of chicken and just chewed at it. All I wanted to do was lay down and rest and stop moving and not puke.

It was the same look I saw on many a face next to me. Sure, there were plenty of people sitting on the grass in the setting sun munching on burgers and chatting about the day's adventures. But there were just as many laying in the shade with that "I will not puke" look that comes from over exertion and too much sun.

Post Script: My mom picked me up and drove me back to my car some 120 miles away. To get to her car on the bike path I had to climb what I could best describe as a half story mound, miniature hill, or an overly ambitious bump in the path.

I walked up it.

After climbing for just under 10 hours with a total day's adventure time of 12 hours, I could not mentally or physically stomach another hill.

Chapter 7

All The Gear You Need

The complete Everyman Tri Gear Review Guide

I was recently poking around the internet statistics for this web site and I noticed that a lot of athletes like to read the race reviews I've written. In fact, a lot of you seek out both race and product reviews. It seems that you are looking for useful information for making purchasing decisions based on what other athletes, such as me, have written about the products (read triathlon toys) that we use and like.

You are looking for insight and critical reviews of the plethora of products and gear that you'll need to purchase to be a successful (or dare I suggest) more successful triathlete.

In a blatant attempt to increase readership, and provide you with my staggering wealth (read best educated guess) here in the complete Everyman Tri Gear Review Guide in race (read swim, bike, and run) order.

The Swim:

1) Goggles:

You need them. If you are like many newbie triathletes, and you've wondering if you do indeed need swim goggles. I can tell you with a great degree of confidences that yes indeed you do need them. I would go even go so far as to suggest that they are pretty important unless you enjoy getting dirty water in your eyes.

Now some of you may be grateful for that hard-earned bit of advice, but a few of you may be wondering to yourself what kind of goggles does the Everyman Triathlete endorse? What brand is the best and provides the most bang for my goggle dollar, euro or yen?

What a great question. And I have a great answer which is ... the kind that don't make you look like Aquaman or Aquawomen. You worked so hard to get that triathlete body so don't spoil it by getting a set of Point Dexter goggles. Basically as any world class swimmer will tell you, it is not about how well you can see out of the goggles, but how good you look in them.

Triathletes in particular have missed the boat on this all important issue and seem to favor massive goggles that look as if they could be worn on a cross country dirt bike adventure. You'll notice that any swimmer, who is anybody, always favors the small Swedish style swim goggle. These are the teeny tiny little goggles, with tiny little rubber straps, that have no rubber insulation between your eyes and the plastic goggle lens.

When worn properly, they only leak about half of the time while providing at best a dirty keyhole view of the underwater world. But that's completely irrelevant as they make any newbie triathlete look like Ian Thorpe, Amanda Beard, or Michael Phelps.

If these names don't ring a bell for you, you should probably stick with the dirt bike über goggles and keep reading.

2) The Wetsuit.

Many newbie triathletes will often ask me if they really need to invest several hundred dollars in a typical triathlon wetsuit. Some will point to the numerous athletes who compete very successfully in their swimsuits.

To answer this question I like to ask another question. Do you enjoy being cold? If the answer to this question is a "yes," the wetsuit is really unnecessary. If you are the type of person that enjoys a good shiver, or if you really like the sound of chattering teeth, or if you really enjoy the feeling wet goose bumps, or if you relish a heart –stopping plunge in frigid water, you may as well skip to the next item.

On the other hand, if don't like any of these, you may seriously consider purchasing a triathlon wetsuit soon.

Some of you may say "while that may be true Roman, you are forgetting the most important part of wearing a wetsuit, that being the positive buoyancy it provides as well as the hydrodynamic benefits thus making the athlete much faster in the water."

"Oh contraire, monsieur," I say to you in my best Pink Panther accent. Because you are forgetting that any potential hydrodynamic benefits a wetsuit provides are easily lost when you try to remove the damn thing on typical sandy beach with your heart rate pounding just a bit north of 200 BPM.

So now that we can agree that a wetsuit is really handy for anybody who likes being warm, you maybe wondering what type or brand of wetsuit I would recommend. I am of course very eager to try out my new 2XU wetsuit as soon as some of the local snow melts.

However did you know that black is the new black? That's right, call me old school but you just can't go wrong with a black wet suit.

A friend of mine recently raced in a very old school wet suit that included some pretty funky nineties neon colors. I just can't help but feel that had he purchased a mostly black wetsuit "in the day" he'd not only still be warm today but also stylin'.

3) Swim Cap:

Many race directors seem to still require them so you might as well get used to wearing one. However I still remember my first race when the guy standing in the water next to me at the start solemnly asked, "You're not gonna wear that black swim cap, are you?"

"I was planning on it," I replied a bit confused.

"You don't want to do that," he added with a knowing nod.

"Why?" I said a bit wide eyed.

"Because they won't see you go down when you drown," he added and swam away.

I looked into the dark murky water where he had been standing and considers this, removed the cap, and threw it to the shore. Only after the race, I realize that I have dark hair.

For swim caps, **white** is the new black.

Next time I review all the important clothes and gear you'll need on the bike portion of the triathlon.

Every day when I get up and check my e-mail I have loads of mail from people around the world seeking my advice. Of course many, if not all, are seeking my advice on how to transfer money from Nigeria, or perhaps how best make a lonely young girl from Russia less lonely here in the United States.

But every-so-often I will get an e-mail that ask something that actually has to do with triathlon, and does not involve the purchase of expensive software or cheap Viagra.

That's why I've created this complete Everyman Tri Gear Review Guide. So let's keep this ball rolling and move right to the bike segment of a triathlon.

4. The Bike:

The bike is without a doubt the most expensive, the most debated, and perhaps the most crucial piece of tri gear. Countless hours and countless words have been written about the pros and cons of the many different types, styles, and brands of bikes available to any aspiring triathlete. Much has been said and debated about the various components, frames, wheels, and even tires that make up the perfect triathlon bike.

Forget all that!

When you really think about it, only one thing really matters on a bike...the paint job. Yes it may seem trivial at first, but if we are really honest with ourselves. it's all about the paint.

To prove my point let me ask you a simple question. Would you buy and ride a really ugly bike? Of course you wouldn't.

Now flip that question around. Would you buy a really cool looking bike even if it didn't have the best components wheels and tires? Of course you would.

Because for the Everyman and Everywomen it not all about how fast we go, but how good we look on the bike. "But Roman, that's so shallow! I think you are dead wrong," you say with righteous indignation.

Let's face it, gang, on any given Sunday most of us are not exactly racing for the podium. So if we can't win, we might as well look like the folks who are winning by having the coolest looking bike in the race. And I'm sure you have noticed that the pros, who do win, always have the coolest looking bikes.

So to sum up the best Everyman bike is one that looks the hottest. Because your bike should say, "even though I'm not leading the field, I could if I decided to really push the pace…so watch out!"

5) The Helmet

Over the last several years the once-simple bike helmet has morphed into an aerodynamic foil of the highest caliber. More and more age-groupers are wearing the same high tech helmets that the pros are wearing. And boy do they look like a bunch of math whiz geeky cone head nerds. It's like they got out their calculators and spent the day figuring out how much easier it would be to make a helmet slight more slippery versus actually getting on the bike and just riding.

What's worse, these very expensive aero helmets start at several hundred dollars and go up in price. Today you can easily spend as much on a carbon aero helmet with a fancy Italian name as on a basic road bike. That's why the Everyman triathlete guide recommends that you go 'old school' when it comes to your choice of helmets.

Do you remember those old leather strap helmets that great riders of the past like Eddie Merckx wore to numerous tour victories? Nothing says that you are hardcore and indeed very serious like a few skimpy leather straps barely tethered to your head.

Unlike all those other "weekend warriors" who wear the wimpy full head helmets, you are ready to risk serious and lifelong brain injury by protecting your head with only a half a dozen flimsy straps of leather.

When the other rider and official eventually ask about the 'old school' head gear just tell them, "if it was good enough for Eddie Merckx, it is certainly good enough for me." And ride away on that hot bike. You can't help but respect anybody willing to risk a life and limb just for a weekend tri.

Plus they'll know that not only are you a bit crazy, but you don't give a damn about the shape of your head, just the size of your thighs.

6) Sun Glasses

Once upon a time it used to be that the more you spent on sunglasses, the better they were. Manufacturers spent a millions developing the best and most precise glass to protect your eyes from every type of solar radiation known to man. Or you would spend the same sum as an entry level Japanese car buying that perfect pair of designer sunglasses that made you look like Christy Brinkley in back in the day when super models were still hot.

Of course within a week you would forget them in a rental car, or your mom would sit on them because you left them on the passenger seat.

So forget about the technology and the designers. Today just about every sunglasses manufacturer has descent plastic solar blocking lens made in China for .99 cents each. On the other hand, if you really want to look like Paris Hilton at a hockey game just wear your designer glasses during a race.

The everyman solution is simple...get a pair of throwaway sports sunglasses You can buy a decent and stylish pair of sunglasses for under $40 at any sports, bike, or Walgreens across the county. Decent sunglasses are just like descent designer watches. Their styles change quickly and the Chinese knock of the new designer styles even quicker.

So get yourself pair of inexpensive sunglasses and when they go out of style, or you leave them in the rent a car, or your mom sits on them, you won't shed any crocodile tears.

7) Bike Shorts

Let's face it. There is just something about the way that bike shorts are designed that make even the tightest and firmest butts look big and for men other body parts look small. Just take a good look at the professional men and women riders of the world and you'll be horrified at how huge their butts look in cycling shorts.

Perhaps it is the way the tight fitting rubber bands of the waits and thighs squeeze the skin making even one percent of body fat bulge and turn into cottage cheese. Or perhaps it is the combination of tight shorts and a tighter bike tops that make the butt just seem so massive in comparison.

Whatever unfortunate optical trick is the cause of this problem the solution is clear….skin toned bike shorts. Not only would these blend with the skin to create a better optical illusion of sheer form and flowing beauty, but they would also be a huge boost to rider safety. You can bet that every driver of every car would now notice the cyclist and gladly share the road just to get a closer look.

For most of us, long before there was swimming and even before there was cycling, there was running. It is what we humans do second. Right after we take those first few tentative steps that take us from baby to toddler, we lean forward and next thing you know, we are running to keep from falling.

So it is with a bit of trepidation that I know turn to running. Never has so much, by so many, been written about such a natural activity. However you'll still need gear. That's why I've created this complete Everyman Tri Gear Review Guide. So let's keep this ball rolling and move right to the run segment of a triathlon.

8) Running Shoes

Buying running shoes at the local running shop may seem straightforward, as it does not require huge amounts of cash, but this too can be deceptive.

You may think that it only requires buying "cool or way cool" running shoes with the correct logo, but wait until they get you on the treadmill. Do you suffer from pronation or supination?

"I have never even heard of these hideous running deformities," you say. But once the sales clerk has you on the treadmill with the video camera running, you'll be amazed at the different types of running shoes for sale to correct this hitherto completely unknown but potentially race-ending deformity.

One hundred and fifty dollars for the top of the line Nike, Brooks or Adidas will seem cheap compared to expensive re-constructive lower leg surgery caused by this problem. So what's the best shoe for you? It is a well known and much discussed fact that certain colors are fast, while others are calming or even slow.

For instance what color is a typical Ferrari?

 Red of course.

What color is a typical semi truck?

White of course.

Now I'm sure we can all agree that a Ferrari is fast while a semi truck is slow. Why? Because a Ferrari is red while a semi is white. For this reason I recommend that you purchase only shoes that of that are red or perhaps shades of red.

Definitely keep away from the calm, soothing or slow colors such as white, green or brown.

Keep in mind that Ferrari's also come in yellow, silver and black. So these are a good second choice of primary colors, should the shoe store be out of the fast red shoes.

9) Sports Watch/GPS/Heart rate monitor

Today's top triathlete all use the latest technology for real time measurement of distance, pace, heart rate, caloric output, and even altitude. The latest in sports watch technology by such manufactures as Garmin, Timex, Polar and even Nike now make it possible to monitor your body and environment like an astronaut on a moon walk.

So what is the best sports watch for the Everyman triathlete?

When you think about it, clock technology has not really advanced much over the last 200 years. Sure you get a few more bells and whistles today but the accuracy of a two-hundred-year-old clock (at least in relative terms) is almost the same as today's modern GPS enabled watch.

Plus today's technology is completely depends on battery life. How many times have you gone for a run only to find that you forgot to charge up your Garmin and that is completely now dead? This makes this modern day time piece about as useful as strapping a dead mouse to your wrist when it comes to keeping time.

That's why I recommend that when it comes to the sports watch you go completely old school. And by old school I mean old old school. I recommend the wind-up grandfather clock. Not only will you never have to worry about battery life but, dragging around a 200-year-old, 25-pound clock on your next training run will not only build character, but high degree of stamina … not to mention wood burns on your skin.

10) Running Clothes

Over the last decade running clothes have evolved from a cotton T-shirts to highly technical moisture-wicking, smelly-bacteria-killing, ultra-light non-rubbing, mega-cooling modern marvels.

I say, "Forget all of this modern crap."

Nothing says that you are very fast and very serious like a black 1970's Led Zeppelin, AC/DC or Iron Maiden concert T-shirt. That's right, the more stuck-out tongues on the concert shirt, the better.

If you really want to be fast you want to exude as much male machismo as possible. And of course nothing says that you are packing a massive piece of endurance hardware like a half-naked photo of a hairy-chested Robert Plant from the greatest heavy metal band (Led Zeppelin) man-handling a massive glittering guitar like Prince at the last Super Bowl.

Of course like with everything in the complex sport of triathlon picking the right band is crucial. The shirt has to be black of course. No other color will do. If you can't find a Led Zeppelin shirt, you can also be fast in shirts that feature bands such as Def Leopard or even the German band, The Scorpions.

But beware; you don't want to fall into the trap of being perceived as a wuss. And nothing says "I'm a wuss" like wearing an 80's hair band shirt. So please please please avoid the 80's hair bands like Motley Crue no matter what you may have heard that Pamela Anderson may or may not have done on camera to Motley Crue band member Tommy Lee.

Triathlon Bling

So you are an aspiring newbie triathlete and you want your neighbors to know. I mean you don't want them thinking that you are just any run-of-the-mill jogger or weekend cyclist. You want to make sure they know that you are living the triathlete dream and soon you'll be featured on network television with heroic feats of endurance on the big island of Hawaii.

Nothing says I'm Kona bound more than triathlon Bling. So for all of you hot young and even aging endurance junkies, here the complete Everyman list of essential triathlon Bling in proper triathlon swim, bike, and run order.

Speedos

Sure, some (especial in the United States) may look at the average tiny Speedo style swim suit and immediately think of a pot-bellied, chain-smoking, furry-backed Frenchmen enjoying his summer holiday on a crowded and dirty beach on some smelly European holiday island. But be that as it may, the tiny Speedo, or TYR or, Nike swim suit is essential triathlon bling.

Why? Because you can't really swim seriously in your typical beach trunks and actually get a decent workout. You can swim like a very angry and drowning cat with your feet churning up the water as you make little to no headway in your drag trunks, but rest assured that no one will mistake you for a triathlete.

Swim Goggles

Somehow it has become chic for newbie triathlete swimmers to wear those massive scuba style goggles. You know the ones I mean: the goggles with one large lens instead of the traditional small swim goggle.

In the best Simon Cowell tradition, I just have to be honest with you here and say that they make even the hottest, hard-body triathlete look like a complete triathlon nerd. Which means that for the rest of us who wear (or have worn) these massive goggles, the jury is in and we're guilty as charged of committing the biggest triathlon fashion faux pas.

So unless you want to be sentenced to a lifetime of triathlon über nerd, get yourself some traditional goggles and just deal with not being able to see so well in the pool.

Areo Bars

Let's face it folks, nothing says to the world "I'm a triathlete" like a set of areo bars on your road bike. Now it would seem obvious that they belong on a road bike, but at last year's Chicago triathlon I did pass a young lady with areo bars on her mountain bike.

Some of you may be wondering, "Hmmm...is it really worth investing in areo bars since I only plan to race one or perhaps two times this year?"

That's a great question, so let me answer it with another great question, "if a tree falls in a forest and nobody is around to hear it fall, does it make a sound?"

In other words, did I tell that young lady at last year's Chicago Triathlon that that she really needed a road bike with areo bars? Of course not!

Did she need a road bike with areo bars? Of course she did.

Bike Pedal Clips

Four words: knee high tube socks.

As in, do you still wear knee high tube socks? Because if you do, I think that you really need to keep those traditional pedals on your bike. Perhaps even keep the old school leather pedal straps, heavy reflector pedal, and really go for newly cool '70s look.

Otherwise you probably want to seriously consider investing in a modern bike shoes, and modern clip-in bike pedals.

Running Shoes

In the not-so-distant past I used to go to my local mall shoe store and purchase either the coolest looking and/or the cheapest on sale running shoe. It would really depend on how much money I was willing to spend to look cool.

Trying out the shoe meant either seeing how it looked with the day's outfit or walking up around the store while the pimpled-faced sales clerk looked like he was impatient to get to his daily Orange Julius break.

When it was all said and done I would shell out just under $100 for a pair of Nikes and walk out of the store wearing them. Inevitably these shoes also became my walking and running shoes until they no longer looked cool.

Today I run (and only run as in not walk around town) in my Saucony Omni Grid something or another shoes (pronounced like sock a knee) and replace them every 300-to-400 hundred miles of running.

I do this because I had a professional fitting done by somebody who actually made me run on a treadmill while recording my running stride with a camera. After playing back the video, the Sauconys seemed to offer the best combination of foot stability and support for me.

Are they cool? Perhaps … now that I've learned how to correctly pronounce the brand name. But what is cool is having healthy feet.

Heart Rate Monitor

Would you drive a car without a fuel gage? Perhaps, but at some point you would inevitably run out of gas.

It's really the same thing with cycling and running without a heart rate monitor. You'll never be able to fine tune your own endurance engine without knowing your heart rate.

So while you bike and run all day without a heart rate monitor, the athlete next to you wearing one has a huge advantage. Besides nothing says I'm a triathlete like fiddling with your watch for 15 minutes before your run trying to get it calibrated correctly to pick up your heart rate.

You neighbors will surely know you are a triathlete just by looking at the massive size of your …. watch.

Chapter 8

TRInspiration

There comes a moment ...

There comes a moment in every race when I think to myself, "Why exactly am I doing this?"

It is usually when the exuberance and adrenaline of the start give way to the realization of just how long and how painful the rest of the race will be.

And let's face it, in a race speed equals pain. In other words, the faster you go, the more it will hurt!

I think that we all know this fact somewhere in the deepest folds of our brains but we tend to hide it, or ignore it, or conveniently misplace it. I do this because if I didn't, I would probably never enter another race again. It is only when I'm actually racing that this realization comes screaming out of its hiding place like a runaway locomotive.

So when this realization inevitably hits the light of day, my brain asks the body, "So how much pain can you tolerate today?" And depending on the amount of training I've done, how I feel that day, the amount of mental energy I have to spend, and how badly I want to succeed and/or win, the answer comes back. And the rest, as they say, is history.

It has taken me six years to even get to this point in my triathlon career. The first year of racing I never had the luxury to make this decision. as it was already made for me. I started training and racing with little regard or knowledge or the sport. It was just something that I thought would be fun to try.

Besides, I thought to myself, how hard can a sprint triathlon really be? It is only a sprint after all.

I figured out the answer to this question on the bike when my legs turned to watery spaghetti at about mile 10 of the 20-mile bike portion of the race. By the time I got to the run, the only decision to be made was how fast I could walk the five miles to save a shred of dignity.

After the race, as I was munching on pizza and slurping beer, I decided that I really liked the sport and that I knew nothing about how to train of race a triathlon.

The following year I threw myself into training and racing. I signed up for every possible race and made every possible mistake in the book. But as I slowly got better, and my endurance improved, I found that I could survive more of the race.

Instead of exploding on the bike, I could now wait until the run to crack like a walnut. The idea of actually racing never really crossed my mind as I just simple wanted to finish an Olympic triathlon running. In other words, not walking any part of the run and actually feeling good crossing the finishing line.

By the end of my second year I had accomplished this so I felt pretty confident when I entered my first half Iron distance race in the spring of my third year of racing.

"How hard can a half Ironman be?" I thought to myself when I entered the race. The answer became painfully obvious on the bike leg as I started to feel sick and weak. By mile ten on the walk I was completely dehydrated, with tunnel vision from heat stroke. It was the first and, so far, the only race that I failed to complete.

By year three of my racing tri career I had a coach. It was my lovely wife that sorted this out and I'll forever be grateful to her and my coach <u>Wes Hobson</u> for this obvious necessity.

I had now spent almost three years trying to reinvent the triathlon training wheel. With the help of Wes I learned more about the sport of triathlon in three months than the previous three years. So much so that I was ready to try my first Ironman distance race. I would have preferred to race an Ironman, but I didn't know that they sell out in about a half an hour.

Sometimes...there comes a moment in racing when your determination to win snaps like an over stretched rubber band.

Do you know that moment?

I can tell exactly when it happens to me. I know the exact instance when my day turns from racing, to surviving, to just wanting to finish.

My first Iron distance race was a bit of train wreck. I had purchased a new bike with an unknown set of problem wheels. So on a hot and muggy race day in Orlando, I spent much of the bike fixing flats.

Eight flats to be exact. My determination to race just kept stretching and stretching and stretching until by the seventh flat it snapped with an audible twang.

I remember sitting at the side of the rode begging the last few racers on the course for a spare tire so that I could fix yet another flat.

A young lady stopped and offered me one of her spare tires which I gladly accepted. She also offered me a peanut butter and jelly sandwich. It was pretty amazing, as she had a steelworker-sized lunch box strapped to the back fender of her bike with a full load of wonderful snacks.

You must remember that at this point in the race I was with a bit more casual bike crowd. The areobar, disk wheel, areo helmet folks were long gone.

I remember saying to her after she offered me the sandwich, "No thanks, I just want to get back on my bike."

And then rethinking and adding "You know ... I will have that sandwich after all. Thank you very much!"

We sat by the side of the road with her munching on cool ranch Doritos and me enjoying a very leisurely PB and J. You could almost hear the snap as I went from wanting to race to just wanting to finish.

It was as if, in the blink of an eye I began to see the fluffy clouds, the bright Florida sun, the austere blue sky, and the boiling black road tarmac.

Before this moment all these things were just props in my play, or variables to be accounted for and forgotten. But now they were real and I was really living in the moment.

Perhaps it is the huge amount of physical exertion of a triathlon that heightens the senses? It is as if every minute becomes an hour and every hour becomes a day, and now I was living and relishing every second.

The pain and the pleasure combine into an intoxicating mixture of life. I could have sat by the side of the road munching on that sandwich forever, but eventually I once again heard the siren call of the finish line. It was time to get back on the bike.

It is funny how focused I become when I race so that the world around me shrinks until it fades into the background. My vision narrows and I only focus on the finish line. But when that rubber band snaps and the world turns back into clear focus, and the sights, sounds, and smells of the day fill my brain with wonder as if I'm drunk on life, that's the moment that I both dread and happily anticipate.

I'm not saying that this is good or bad. It is just different and stark contrast between racing and just wanting to finish is so vivid that when this happens in a race, I always know.

Sometimes there comes a moment in racing when your determination to win snaps like an over stretched rubber band.

Do you know that moment?

Those 17 Unforgettable Hours

There is no magic in the number 140.6. It represents a very random distance that several guys in Hawaii came up with in the winter of 1978 to determine if a swimmer, cyclist, or runner is the best endurance athlete.

U.S. Navy Commander John Collins (one of the Hawaii guys who began it all) is widely quoted as saying, "Whoever finishes first, we'll call him the Iron Man."

And so the first Ironman race took place on the small island of Oahu in the winter of 1978 with a 2.4 mile swim, a 112 mile bike ride (the distance around the island) and a traditional running marathon of 26.2 miles.

From Wikipedia, "Of the fifteen men to start off the in early morning on February 18th, 1978, twelve completed the race. Gordon Haller was the first to earn the title Ironman by completing the course in a time of 11 hours, 46 minutes, and 40 seconds."

It is worth noting here that athletes were completely self-supported. More importantly, handwritten on the last page of the very sparse three sheets of paper listing a few rules and a course description was this exhortation: "Swim 2.4 miles! Bike 112 miles! Run 26.2 miles! Brag for the rest of your life!" This is now the Ironman registered trademark.

It is also the heart and soul of the Ironman. Over the last decade, as Ironman racing has expanded throughout the world, the distance of 140.6 has become etched in stone as the mystical number that represents an Ironman.

It has become so synonymous with the Ironman that the number, divided by half, and now trademarked (70.3) represents it own racing series. Athletes around the world aspire to complete both the shorter and longer distance as a way to prove their status as the top endurance dog.

But to me the real magic is not in this random number, but in the journey and ultimate goal to complete the Ironman. Let's just pretend for a second that Oahu was 20 miles bigger or even 20 miles smaller. Would the numbers 120.6 or 160.6 be any more or less significant than 140.6?

Or we could easily imagine that during the marathon at the 1908 Olympic Games in London the course was **not** extended at the last minute by 385 yards from its set 26 miles so that the runners would cross the finish line in front of the royal family's viewing box in the Olympic arena.

If the course extension had not happened in 1908, that would make today's Ironman only 140.4 miles long. Is this number any more or less significant?

The answer is that the number in itself is really irrelevant. What counts is what was written on that last piece of paper almost 20-years ago before the start of the first Ironman: "Brag for the rest of your life."

When you think about it, the vast majority of us age-group athletes will never even come close to matching or even breaking that first self-supported course time of 11 hours, 46 minutes, and 40 seconds.

It is not about a winning time.

It is not about the distance.

It is not about the number 140.6

It is about the last hours of the journey of reaching to what many age-group triathletes seems like an almost unattainable goal of finishing an Ironman ... in less than 17 hours. That why I would argue that the number 17 is really the magic number in any Ironman.

It is the last 17 critical hours of all the weeks, months and perhaps years of training that only matter in the end. All of the other previous hours spent in the pool, on the bike, on the run are now just so much water under the bridge.

It is the 17 dawn to midnight race hours when your hopes and dreams are final realized, or dashed on the jagged rocks of the swim, bike run.

It is those 17 magical hours that all of your daily worries, cares, concerns fade into the far background and you become laser focused on just one goal: Finishing before midnight.

It is the 17 heroic hours when you feel your body rise to the challenge of pushing yourself longer than you have ever imagined possible.

It is the 17 wonderful hours when life and limitless energy course through your veins, chiseling your body into the ultimate endurance machine.

It is the 17 dreaded hours when emotionally you climb the highest of highs and fall with a huge thud into the lowest of lows.

It is in the 17 unbelievable hours when pushing yourself beyond the breaking point is just the start of your day.

It is those 17 crazy hours when time simultaneously expands and contracts. When seconds become hours, and days turn into minutes.

It is the 17 momentous hours that to a great extent will define all of the following hours of your life.

It is in the 17 crucial hours when you really learn if you are made of Iron or not.

When I completed my first Iron distance race I told my buddy how far I swam, biked and ran. He kind of just stared at me. I could tell the distance numbers were pretty meaningless to him.

Unless you've actually swam, ridden, or ran for fairly long way (which he had not) 10 miles or 100 miles are pretty much the same to you. So instead, I mentioned that it took me almost 17 hours to finish the race.

His eyes exploded open in disbelief. "You mean you raced for an entire day and night," he said, stunned as the idea of exercising all day and night really sank in.

It was only in those 17 unforgettable hours that I had earned the right to brag for the rest of my life!

There is no such thing as an easy Ironman

I'm always amazed at how much gnashing of teeth and wringing of hands goes on in picking the first Ironman race. Considering that most of the North American races sell out in about 2.5 seconds, just getting into a race should be the main concern. But inevitably new Ironman athletes pick a race based on the difficulty of the race.

That's why Ironman Florida always gets a huge number of newbie Ironman athletes. Over the years it has earned the reputation as one of the easiest races on North America and perhaps even the world. The common mis-belief is that the dead flat bike (OK one bridge on the course does not a hill make) and run make it the perfect newbie race.

So for all of you newbies signed up for the race this year I would suggest that you sit back and take a deep breath because I've got some bad news for you: there is no such thing as an easy Ironman. They are all very hard!

This notion of an easy IM is just something that newbies use to psych themselves up for doing the race. Think of it as a coping mechanism that enables triathletes to go online a year before the race and slam down their credit for 500 big bucks and sign up for their first IM.

The thinking goes something like this, "I want to do an Ironman, but I'm not sure I can do it, so why not start with the easiest one of the bunch." This way the thought of swimming 2.4 miles, followed by a 112-mile bike ride, followed by a marathon seems almost reasonable. "Sure it is an Ironman, but it's an easy Ironman," the rationalization goes.

You still have to cover 140.6 miles and do it in less than 17 hours.

Did you know that after last year's Florida Ironman an age-group athlete was barely clinging to life from fighting the five-foot seas and strong currents on the swim portion of the race.

I was there and I can tell you that while swimming is my strongest discipline of the big three (I've gone 1:10 in my best Ironman), I would have seriously thought twice before jumping into the rough Gulf Coast waters on that extremely windy and cold morning.

For argument's sake, let's ignore the rough seas, cold waters, and rip currents on the swim course and move on to the bike. (BTW: I witnessed athletes pulled hundreds of yards of course by these currents.)

The bike portion is, after all, why most folks consider this to be an easy IM.

First of all, how many of you have ever run a downhill marathon? Please raise your hand. I have and I can tell you that it was the worst marathon of my life. My initial thinking for picking the Top of Utah marathon was that it would be blazingly fast and easy. After all, the first 19 or so miles are all downhill through an absolutely gorgeous canyon. How hard can it be to run downhill for 19 miles, I thought when I clicked submit on my computer entry?

Boy, was I ever wrong!

By mile 19 my thighs were completely blown and my legs felt like spaghetti. What followed was the worst, most painful, 10K my life. All of the time I had made up at the start of the marathon, quickly evaporated as I dragged my spongy legs across the last 10K of the race.

There is a good reason why London and Chicago are considered the fastest marathons. It is because the course in sections is flat and/or gently rolling. The perfect combination for lighting fast times that allows runners to use/mix and match all of their leg muscles and not just their thighs. Also both races are also held at normally cool times of the year which are perfect for fast running times.

Just like the Top of Utah marathon, the Florida bike course has only one grade for the bike…pancake flat. That means that for 112-miles you get to sit on your bike in the areo-position watching the Wal-Marts, weeds and Waffle Houses fly by as you peddle using the exact same muscles for every painful revolution. There is no climbing, and there is no coasting. There is no change what-so-ever to the course, so there is no change to your body position.

There is however the changing headwind. Last year is howled at over 20 mph for most of the morning and afternoon. This meant that many racers reported fighting a headwind for the entire bike portion of the race.

It did die down in the early afternoon.

That was about just that time that sun came blazing out, the humidity spiked, and most athletes started the marathon.

I must be honest here and report that at about that time I was happily sitting in an air-conditioned Starbuck sipping on a lovely cold ice tea. I remember thinking to myself as I watched the sweaty and over-heated patrons come into the Starbucks, "self, it would really suck to have to run a marathon about now."

Just a quick word here about the IM Florida marathon course … to call it boring would be like calling Howard Stern tame. The course rambles its way through some of the strip mall -like streets of Panama City until it takes a sharp turn through several trailer parks into the "scenic" garden portion of the course. Let's just leave it at saying that it is no Chicago, New York, London, or Berlin marathon course.

In fact the race headquarters of the Florida Panama City IM seems to smack a bit of that sleazy and rundown feel of an MTV spring break destination. I suppose that this is because it is a huge sleazy and run down college Spring Break destination. This is all well and good, unless it happens to be completely devoid of spring breakers, which of course it is in November.

This means that on course, and when you cross the finish line, you will only be greeted by a few hardcore IM family and friends. There is no crowd support; there are no throbbing masses of well wishers. All you get are a few pissed-off locals on their way to the Waffle House, who don't understand why they have to wait to cross the street for a bunch of sweaty and stinky runners.

Oh yea, I almost forgot. You also get to run next to a virtual parade of loud pick-up trucks, Harleys, and red neck Riviera types.

For all of you finished the race, and all of you who attempted the race, be very proud of your accomplishment. If you crossed the finish line in under 17 hours you have more than earned the words, "You are an Ironman!"

And for all of you signed-up for the race this year; please train hard, because there is no such thing as an easy Ironman: They are all very hard!

To race or not to race, that is the question

I recently received a note from a athlete who is going through a very tough time. She was well beyond the point of when it rains it pours. After a recent divorce, bankruptcy, and illness, she was questioning her commitment to race her first half Ironman this year.

And who could blame her? As you well know, as the race gets longer, so does the training. One hour fun runs turn into three hour slogs. A nice and easy 20-mile bike ride turns into a must do 80-mile butt burn. The weekly swim quickly becomes a 3000-yard Masters Swimfest at least three times a week.

And not only does the training increase in both intensity and duration, but the cost and complexity of the race also dramatically sky rockets. Who among you all can tell me right here and now what goes in all five race bags during the standard Ironman ordeal?

Or who here has spent hours and/or days just trying to get to race? Traveling with a bike has all the grace and elegance of traveling with your baby pet elephant. The only difference is that the typical airline gate clerk can probably actually check in your elephant without making you open and unpack it.

So what did I tell her?

Sometimes the best thing you can do is not race.

When all your training seems to be going downhill…

When you don't feel the passion, just the pain…

When you can't focus or find the fun…

When your heart and head can't agree…

When the race becomes a burden, and the burden gets to be too heavy…

When your head says yes, but your injured body screams,"no more"…

When you see only the trees and never the forest…

When the other side of the mountain turns brown…

When your heart turns cold…

When your bike gets dusty…

When you days are just too short…

When your family, friends or God need you most…

Sometimes the best thing you can do is not race.

So what did I tell her?

Sometimes the best thing you can do is race.

When everything else in life is falling to bits…

When you feel like you have no control over your family, work, eating or health…

When you have so very little to look forward to when you wake up in the morning…

When you need something to jump start your day…

When you need conquer something that seems unconquerable…

When you need a reason to hit the path, pool, and road…

When you want to sleep like there is no tomorrow…

When you want to feel the real power of your muscles and lungs…

When you need to feel in total control of a few precious minutes of the day…

That's when you have to close your eyes, make a mental fist, and determine that you will go the entire distance no matter what life puts in your way.

You will sweat…

You will suffer…

You will swear…

You will survive and cross that finish line.

You don't know or care what awaits you on the other side of that line because right now, this instance, the next few hours, days, weeks, and months ... the finish line is all that matters.

So what did I tell her?

I wrote back and said that she must absolutely do the race. Sometimes a race can not only become a goal, but indeed is the only goal worth accomplishing.

Chapter 9

Long Course World Championships

Up and Over Down Under (part 1)

Australia is really far away from Colorado.

Now this may sound like an obvious statement, but to understand what it really means you'll have to fly thousands of miles in my shoes on a United Airlines flight packed to the brim with passengers.

You know it is a very long way when…

- You've watched five movies and you still have several hours of flight time left.

- You leave home on a Saturday afternoon and arrive in Sydney on a Monday morning.

- You are served three meals, several snacks and countless rounds of those lukewarm, moist, flaccid towlettes meant to refresh and cleanse.

By the way I'm always a little freaked out when they come to collect the used towlettes and they refuse to use their hands to collect them, instead they use the little plastic salad tongs. It is like they don't really trust me to use the towlette to wipe the "correct" part of my body, if you know what I mean.

But I've sugar-coated the experience long enough. Flying economy on United Airlines sucks. And flying economy on a aging and overused United long haul 747 for over 14 hours sucks beyond description, but I'll give describing it try nevertheless.

Recently I read Airbus was experimenting with a new passenger restraining system aboard its brand new über-jumbo plane that would allow passengers (read cattle) to fly standing up. This would let the airlines pack up to 30 percent more people aboard the plane, which by the way, is already designed to fly as many as 555 passengers.

Image how much fun flying on this beast will be when you have to load and unload 555 people with all their stuff, issues and smells.

Speaking of issues, we almost missed our flight because a woman with more tattoos and piercings than your average rain forest headhunter freaked out on the connecting flight to LA because she was overcome by strange odors from the back of the plane. After a long and very public five-minute hug from the captain in the middle of the aisle, we had to taxi back to the gate to allow her and her "issues" to depart the plane.

Now multiply this incident by 555 and you've got a fun day of travel once the new über–sized airbus starts flying around the USA.

But I digress. I was explaining how airbus was working on packing 30 percent more people into a plane by allowing them to stand up during the flight. Well it seems that United, at least in economy class, has already accomplished this by stacking people horizontally instead of vertically, just like tumbled-down.

On this long haul 747's, when the person in front of you reclines their seat, they are pretty much up close and very personal with you and your lap. Now this could be a good thing if done at the right time (late at night), in the right place (bedroom), with the right person (your sexy spouse or girl/boyfriend or eager new friend), with the right amount of clothing (none).

But instead you end up with Jed, or Mohammed, or the perfect stand-in for your crazy, fat and hated aunt from Rochester lying in your lap for 14 hours, while you lie in Jed's or Mohammed's or your crazy fat aunt's lap.

Either way this makes for a total no-win situation. Imagine taking a Greyhound bus from LA to New York with perhaps a tad bit better dental hygiene on the part of your questionable fellow passengers (or cattle as the airlines call us when we're not listening), and you get the idea.

Thus I arrived in Sydney on a beautiful Monday morning feeling as if I had just been severely violated in numerous and unholy ways by the bad boys of the prison chain gang.

Australia is indeed a stunning and beautiful country. There are many wonderful and positive observations you can say about a place the same size as the continental United States with only about 30 million inhabitants. I'll leave those things to the travel guides. Instead here are just a few of my personal observations from the very limited time I spent Down Under.

Australia's economy seems to be based exclusively on two things:

1) The buying/selling/making and consuming of coffee.
2) The buying/selling and brokering of real estate.

On every street corner, on every city in Australia, you'll find either a real estate office or a coffee shop. I suspect that a typical conversation in Australia must go something like this, "G'day mate, let's buy a new home and get some coffee."

"Ah what a great idea mate, I could use a new place and a creamy rich macchiato."

Indeed if you were to chart the modern Australian economy 40 percent would be coffee sales, with and additional 40 percent going to the real estate sector. The remaining 20 percent would be allocated to the production of cute and cuddly stuffed kangaroos, wombats and koalas.

And just like in the United States 100 years ago, the real animals are either shot as vermin (kangaroos), or poisoned as pests (wombats) or run over by speeding cars (koalas). It's good to know that we still lead the way in the world in so many environmental initiatives.

I wonder how many more years it will take Australia to follow in our footsteps and completely slaughter all of their indigenous animals just as we did with our buffalo, grizzlies and wolves?

But I prefer to look on the bright side of things. Once all of the indigenous animals are gone, Australia will be able to reintroduce a smaller and hopefully much smarter population of kangaroos, wombats and koalas back into the wild thus creating an entire new industry and finally diversifying their economy beyond coffee, real estate and stuffed cute animal production.

Up and Over Down Under (part 2)

Sydney ranks high among the world's most beautiful coastal cities. If you were to pen a short list of the best ocean side cites, Sydney would be competing for top place with cities like Vancouver, Paris, and San Francisco.

These were my thoughts as I sat on the city tour bus the day after we arrived in Sydney. It was cold and pissing-down rain, so the inside of the bus was especially warm and comfy.

Today there would be no hopping off this bus and onto another bus at any of Sydney's many tourist attractions. Instead I just sat smugly on the bus and watch the people outside scurry from shelter to shelter and still get completely soaked like wet poodles in a torrential downpour of Biblical proportions.

But what really sealed the deal for me and put Sydney on the top of a very short list of the world's greatest cities was that inbetween pointing out this famous bridge and that historical building, dock or landmark, the tour conductor also pointed out the many Olympic 50 meter pool complexes in and around Sydney.

In fact I soon came to learn that you can't swing a dead kangaroo (BTW: the rare albino roo pictured is not dead, just sleeping, for all you who happen to be wondering) in Australia without hitting a 50 meter pool. Which for somebody like me, who took up swimming late in life and thus has only known the pain of swimming back and forth and back and forth like some deranged and crazed guppy in a 25-yard pool, is brilliant (as the Aussies like to say) and as close to swim heaven as you can get.

What makes the plethora of 50-meter pools especially appealing in Australia is that they are dirt cheap to use. From an American perspective, Australia has become an expensive place to holiday since the USD became the sinker in the world's currency toilet.

I quickly learned that Australia, for us Americans, is like living and shopping and eating at the airport. Everything you need is readily available for about 50 percent more than you think it should cost. Almost everything in Australia is "airport expensive" for Americans.

As an example I don't think that our small family of three ever ate out at any nice restaurant for under $70 U.S. A better example might be our highway lunch stop at the local Hungry Jack's (that would be Burger King to you and me, Cowboy) where our lunch special meal of three Hungry Jack "Feeds" (and what an appropriate name) came to just under $30 Aussie dollars or about $25 USD.

Now contrast this with the $2.50 Aussie fee I paid in Port Macquarie to swim in the local 50-meter pool, and you'll see that swimming in Australia is a bang-on bargain. I suspect that this is because

swimming in Australia is one of the biggest and most followed national sports.

In fact I have never been to a country that is more swim crazy. When Ian Thorpe announced his retirement, it was national news for over a week. And the rumor and speculation of his pending retirement was the top national story for the weeks prior to the actual announcement.

I can't even beginning to express how wonderful it is to be in a place were the discussion of swimming, instead of terrorism, war and death, dominates the national psyche. I can tell you that in all of the towns I visited I was able to swim at a 50-meter pool day or night. What further astounded me was the plethora of Masters classes available for swimmers of my meager ability.

In Australia they call masters "Squad" and unlike here in the States, they actually have three (can you believe it) different types of squads. In Sydney at the local pool they had the following squad swims:

1) Traditional Swimming Squad (This was similar to a U.S. masters classes)

2) Triathlon Squad (Specifically designed for triathletes. We did longer swims along with swim/run workouts around the pool)

3) Open Water Squad (Specifically for open water ocean swimmers with an emphasis on skills like being able to dive under waves and dealing with rough water)

Australia must surely be the place that old swimmers go when they swim into the sunset.

Some of you may be thinking, "So what's the big deal about swimming in a 50 meter pool?"

It is like the difference between showering at your first cheap post-college apartment, and showering in one of those gold-plated, six-head palace showers you see installed in multi-million dollar homes on Home and Garden television. Both showers will get you wet and clean, but you look forward to the fancy one.

A better way to describe it might be to image a typical 200-meter masters swim. In my current pool that means swimming about 9 lengths of my pool. You start swimming; you get into a good groove, and guess what? You have to turn and turn and turn! In a 50-meter pool, 200 meters means only four lengths of the pool. You just swim, and swim, and swim, and swim some more And eventually you hit a wall. But by the time you get to it, you're over the moon

to see it, as you need a bit of rest from all that swimming. At least that's how I felt swimming triathlon squad in Sydney.

Plus the Andrew "Boy" Charlton Pool was beyond amazing. They had actually built it to float over one of the city's many scenic bays (right next to Sydney's botanical gardens) with countless tree-lined meandering trails and paths. This meant I could go for a beautiful four--mile run through the city's botanical gardens, along the ocean and around the Opera House, jump into the pool for a bit of swim, and then sip a truly spectacular cappuccino at the pool's café. Did I mention that almost half of the Australian economy is based on coffee?

Can you think of a more wonderful workout? No wonder the Australian are such a huge power house in the sports of swimming and triathlon. If I had the time and money I would make this run/swim/coffee my daily routine.

Wouldn't you?

Up and over Down Under (part 3)

What do you call a bunch of triathletes strutting around in their national race kit in the lobby of an

old Australian hotel like peacocks on display?

You call it the USA team meeting a few days before the 2006 ITU long course world championships.

I was amazed and honestly a bit embarrassed by the spectacle. My wife and I decided that it was best to stay in the team hotel, as we were new to this entire world championship business. Basically the now defunct long course distance was about two-thirds the length of an Ironman race.

The World Championship moves around every year and my wife had qualified at the Great Floridian Triathlon the year before in Florida. Now I have to be honest here and point out that most of the world's best Iron Distance triathletes aim for the Ironman World Championship held in Kona Hawaii every year.

The ITU (International Triathlon Union) sanctions most of the Olympic distance races throughout the World, but the long course or "Ironman" distance races are really better attended and in effect owned by Ironman. So while technically this was the world championship in the long course triathlon, most triathletes would consider it a somewhat distant second to the Kona race.

However, this in no way takes away from any of the athletes competing for their country in what turned out to be a very challenging race … that is, unless they happened to be strutting around like peacocks in their team kit that Friday morning in Canberra.

Canberra (pronounced Can-bra by most locals) is Australia's reluctant capital. It was chosen as the capital as a compromise between Sydney and Melbourne. It happens to be about halfway between both cities and in the middle of pretty much nowhere. It is a highly planned city with beautiful wide boulevards, well-manicured parks, and lovely manmade lakes. It also happens to be almost impossible to walk around the city center without crossing 25 wide boulevards with speeding cars all coming at you from the wrong direction, at least if you are from a country where you drive on the right side of the road.

Canberra is clean, tidy, completely manicured and devoid of anything that might smack of character. It's the kind of place where you drink too much just to forget all of the places that you would rather be at. And drinking too much was exactly what I was doing at a local English-style pub. We had now been in Australia for almost a week and we had not seen one freaking kangaroo. And that was all my son really cared about seeing in Australia, anyway.

We had spent hours on the drive to Canberra looking for the mysterious beast. Every so often my wife would yell out in great surprise as she has spotted what she thought was a kangaroo with her Lasik eagle eyes. When we got closer, the kangaroos turned out only to be very energetic cows, sheep or windblown bushes.

So it came as a complete surprise when the pub proprietor told us that we could see a bunch of the elusive beasts just a short walk from the pub. And by

surprise I mean one of those "no duh" moments that I know so well from my home in Colorado.

You see, I live just a short distance away from Rocky Mountain National Park. And every fall we get billions of tourists from around the nation and world that descend upon Estes Park to see the Elk rut. For you and me that would be the elks' mating season when the big-horned bulls come down from the mountains and bugle their lust across the vast expenses of the park. The really big and successful bulls must gather and defend a harem of females from the horny young bucks. As you would imagine, a regular animal planet show ensues with all of the frightening drama and sex that nature can provide, free of charge.

All this happens mostly at the local golf course. Which of course is a shame, because all of the billions of tourist with their high powered binoculars and expensive digital cameras are crowed in the park eager to visually assault anything that remotely looks like an elk in heat.

I, on the other hand, am having a really hard time making my approach shot to the 18th hole at the Estates Park Public Golf Course because I have to shoot over a humping elk hazard. And I'm already well over par because I have yet to find a golf club that is specifically designed to blast a ball from a steaming mound of elk dung. And believe me there's a lot of steaming piles all over the course, as these animals eat the lush grass of the 18th hole, instead of the tough scrubby grass in the national park.

So it came as no surprise when the pub's bar tender told me to go up the hill and take a look for the elusive Kangaroos at the local golf course. And sure as Elk dung, we were treated to the sight of dozens of Kangaroos feeding, paying, hopping, skipping and humping, all over the 18th fairway.

Once again these smart animals found the lush soft grass of the local golf course, a much preferred alternative to the scrubby, sandy, and heat-baked dry land of the surrounding hills.

When will I learn?

After snapping a few digital photos of the kangaroos, we returned to our hotel for the athletes' parade. When I had read about the parade I imagined

something like we are used to here on the Fourth of July or perhaps the pageantry of the Rose Bowl, or the spectacle of the Macy's Day Parade in New York.

Basically we stood around downtown for an hour waiting for some mysterious signal to start marching. This was after milling about for two hours waiting for the official USA team photo to be snapped. Imagine the hilarity trying to get about a dozen friends lined up for a photo. Now multiply that hilarity by a factor of 10, and you've got the makings of a two-hour photo shoot for the official USA race picture.

The parade was a lot of fun in the sort of way that walking down the street with a few hundred of your best friends would be. At one point we walked by somebody with what looked like a very serious video camera so we yelled USA, number 1, and anything else we could remember from the Olympic television coverage and waved the red white and blue banner for all of Canberra to appreciate on the evening news.

About a mile into the parade it turned into an unorganized leisurely walk and we decided to abandon the entire thing for a carbohydrate-laden pre-race dinner. As happens at most races, we were only able to find overcrowded and over priced Italian restaurant that server what could best be described as uninspired spaghetti at a very inspired price.

What is it about spaghetti that has made it the ubiquitous choice for any and all endurance races of any sort? I guess I wasn't looking when somebody crowned the noodle king as the mandatory pre-race menu . And that's a shame, as I have yet to have even a remotely interesting or memorable pre-race spaghetti dinner. It tends to be a somewhat nervous and twitch affair that is crowned by the serving of the soggy noodle and mushy tomato, eaten with an equally soggy plastic fork on a flaccid paper plate.

And so it was with this meal, except that we paid for the privilege with the Aussie dollars. I suppose this pre-race ritual has now become so ingrained in my brain that it now carries with it a bit of excitement, as I know that in just a few short restless evening hours, we race.

Chapter 10

The Everyman Hat Trick ... Three Races In One Month

The Secret Sauce

I have a friend by the name of Martin who is an exceptional endurance athlete. I say endurance athlete and not triathlete because he is an exceptional swimmer, cyclist, and long distance runner.

Just to give you an idea of his level of talent, I've never seen him place outside of the top ten in any given race he has entered. And that includes triathlons, marathons and long distance swim events. He almost always wins his age group and believe me that is saying a lot in a city like Boulder that is stuffed to the rafters with highly talented endurance athletes.

So what's his secret? What's the secret sauce that makes him such a winner?

I think I figured it out this weekend on a long, easy run with my dog.

For instance, just like my dog, Martin makes running look effortless. I kind of plod along, shaking and rattling the ground with my heavy heel strikes while Happy, my dog, just effortlessly trots along next to me looking like she could do this all day and night.

Martin has that same sort of easy and happy-go-lucky running style. He can easily run a sub 2:45 marathon while looking like he's taking a stroll through the park on a lazy Sunday afternoon.

But that's not the secret sauce. I think that has more to do with natural genetic talent and years of hard training. I really believe that if we put in the time, we can all look effortless in any given endurance sport. In the case of running our genetics may not allow us run sub-six-minute miles, but we can certainly run sub-seven- or even sub-eight-minute miles, and make it look easy.

So what is the secret sauce that makes Martin such a winner?

I believe it's the same stuff that athletes like Lance Armstrong possesses in spades. It is the ability to put it all together come race day. This intangible ability is what separates the great ones from the rest of us weekend warriors. It is the ability to harness all of those hours of training and preparation and consistently raise your game to the next level when you need it the most.

I sometimes swim with a guy at masters who always likes to say that racing gets in the way of his training. In other words he loves to train, but hates to race. He says that he swims for the pure love of swimming and that racing would get in the way of his pursuit. I completely understand what he is saying, especially when I'm standing at the edge of the water before a big race. I think to myself "what's the point of all of this pressure," as my stomach does somersaults from all of the tension. "Wouldn't it be enough just to swim for the pure love of swimming or run just for the pure love of running?" I wishfully consider just before the guns sounds the start of yet another hard effort.

But once the race starts, and I get past the initial few moments of panic and I start to feel the strength and power of my muscles and lungs, I understand why **not** racing can never be an option for me. Because I love racing! However, unlike my friend Martin, I cannot consistently put it all together for a winning effort on race day.

I suppose at this point it would be important to define what winning effort means for me because it has changed over the years.

When I first started racing triathlons, a winning effort simply meant finishing the race. It seemed like a simple enough goal just to drag my tired and cramping body across the finish line. It really didn't matter if I came in first or last. I just wanted to finish.

The problem with this goal is (at least for me) that if you set the goal low, the reward tends to be low. I would finish a race feeling tired and not all that happy. Sure I had finished, but certainly not in a time or place I could tell my friends about and certainly not with a lot of style. Dragging my sorry butt across the finishing line while looking like a pale and sick turtle was not something to brag about.

So my goal changed. It evolved from just wanting to finish to wanting to finish strong. To me it meant being able to finish a triathlon running.

Now my old coach Wes Hobson would say that's not really a goal, since you can't measure it and you certainly can't quantify it. And he's right. A smart goal needs to something that is reachable, attainable and most importantly measurable.

By my second year of racing I was able to finish a triathlon running, but I still wasn't satisfied. So I set a new goal: To just finish my first Ironman. You think I would have learned by now. I was able to finish the Ironman, but it was like my triathlon. Dragging my tired butt across the finish line was great, but something was still missing.

And then it happened for the first time last year at the Chicago Triathlon I got a hold of some of that secret sauce and to my complete amazement I was actually racing for position. And the experience of actually racing was like nothing I had ever dreamt about. It was so much fun that I could not stop smiling for a week. Who would have thought that Lance had so much fun leading a race? At least I hope he did.

It was fantastic to be fighting it out for the podium, even though I didn't realize it at the time. I only knew I was racing a guy in my age-group to finish.

As usual after the race I went for a nice lunch with some good friends. It wasn't until I got back home to Boulder that another friend told me they had called out my name at the awards ceremony. That must be a mistake I thought, but it wasn't. I had taken second in my race category and it felt terrific. Who would have known that the secret sauce is not only less filling, but tastes great?

So now I'm completely hooked. I want that feeling of putting it all together on race day for a winning performance again.

I don't just want to finish.

I don't just want to finish strong.

I want to be a winner!

And that really means that the hard work has just begun.

There's always something … Chicago Triathlon

There is always something that goes wrong at every race. There is always an excuse for any type of performance.

My total official race count is now well into the triple digits and I can promise you that for me at least there is no such thing as a perfect race.

Indeed in my eyes the real test of an athlete is not how they perform when all is going well, but how they handle themselves when the day gets on the fast train and heads south.

So with this in mind, here are all of my race excuses, travails, and mishaps that marked my third attempts at the Chicago Accenture International Triathlon. Perhaps some of them will sound familiar to you.

Excuse # 1: Hours of sitting

When I was driving from Boulder to Chicago with my race buddy, Dave, I couldn't help but point out the nifty navigation system in my little electric hybrid car.

"Look Dave," I said pointing to the navigation screen. "That's highway number 74, the one that goes to Peoria. But why are we on it?" I added, a bit confusedly, as I looked out the window.

"Hey, we're in Peoria," I almost shouted with a sudden realization that I had just driven us about two hours south instead of north to Chicago.

Dave was not amused, as you can imagine, since we had just spent something like 1,800 hours sitting in a car before his only race of the year and my "A" race of the season.

Excuse # 2: Going too hard on a training workout right before the race

To make up for too much time spent in the car, we decided to go for an easy run on Friday night to shake out the cramps from being in the car for two days as I had now been cramped up in the car for two days straight.

We started out slowly, but about a mile into the wooded run in the Chicagoland forest preserve, we met up with a really ticked-off skunk. He was by the side of trail with his tail up, locked and loaded for some spraying action.

I asked Dave, "How far can a skunkspray?" He said, "About 15 feet."

 For some reason I figured he should know because he's a doctor, and after all and they deal with skunks all the time or at least that's how my thinking went.

Our trail was about four feet wide with little-to-no room to go around Pepé Le Pew. Dave graciously let me go around the skunk first. I went around and waited for Dave.

But unfortunately for Dave, his clever plan "backfired," as the skunk was really angry now and decided to take it out on the guy behind him. It would not let Dave pass. As he moved to the right side of the path so did the skunk. As he moved to the left side of the path so did the skunk.

It wasn't until I almost laughed so hard that I peed myself that Dave, with a superhuman burst of speed, managed to get around the critter safe and smell-free.

But the damage had been done. Our adrenaline was now pumping and we pounded the rest of the six-mile run way too hard for a being just about 36 hours out from our race.

Later on the run we were passed on the trail by a mountain biker who brought with him more than just a whiff of angry skunk stink!

Excuse # 3: Poor eating and upset stomach

The next day at the Chicago Tri Expo, Dave and I decide to graze on the free samples, as we somehow forgot about lunch. Perhaps I had forgotten about lunch because after our skunk adventure I decided to carbo load with a rack of ribs at one my favorite Chi-Town rib joints. Did you know that ribs were a great source of carbs when eaten in Chicago?

Anyway I freely mixed free samples of this and that carb / protein / hydration / nutrition / recovery drink with free samples of chocolate/ caramel /vanilla / raisin / oatmeal / chocolate chip / bar for a deadly gastrointestinal cocktail.

Excuse # 4: Too much time on my feet before the race

So, on top of this stomach bomb, I decided that Dave might be interested in seeing the city and the course from a bird's-eye view. Dave's a good Kansas boy, so I though I'd impress him with my hometown's skyscraper architecture.

So we set of from the Hilton to the John Hancock building's 94th observatory floor on foot. This turned out to be a one-hour expedition down Michigan Avenue that involved the crossing of thousands of busy streets, a river, and fighting our way through the hoards of shoppers on Michigan Avenue's one magnificent mile.

We arrived tired, dehydrated, and disheveled. The view of the city and the race course was spectacular, but the damage to my race day had been done.

Excuse # 5: Lack of sleep

The night before the race I managed to stay up until 11 p.m., watching a movie with my high school friends. Somehow the fact that I had to get up a 4 a.m. to get to the transition area escaped me.

In fact I would have loved to have had five hours of sleep. But after I went to bed, a noisy neighbor kept blabbing on his deck just outside my window and I didn't manage to fall asleep until well after midnight.

Excuse # 6: Technical problem

To my absolute horror when I went to blow up my rear tire on my bike, I noticed that I could not get any air into it. What had happened? When you have a full or partial disk wheel like I use, you also need valve extenders. These are little extenders on the valves that make it possible to blow up the tire.

I suspect that the little screw on my valve had closed itself (you leave this open when using valve extenders) and so I couldn't get any air into the rear tire. To make matters worse coming from altitude at Colorado I was already down on air pressure, as we have less air there to begin with.

My choice was to take the tire off and fix it, or race with it as is. I went with racing as is, so I suspect I raced with about only 70 pounds in my rear wheel. It was a bit squishy and certainly a bit slower.

Excuse # 7: Terrible wave start position

In fact I was in the worst possible wave, dead last. OK, I'm not being completely honest here, the relay teams were behind me, but as far as individual competitors go I was dead last.

Wave number 51 was my Clydesdale wave.

That meant that I started a full four hours after transition closed at 5:45 a.m., with nothing to do but get nervous and wait in huge lines for the pathetically few bathrooms that Capri Events (the race organizers) provided for the 8,000 athletes.

Thank heaven for the company of fellow raceAthletes Bigun, Dave and Tim, to name just a few who waited with me for their waves to start.

Excuse # 8: Capri and Timberline Timing.

I could have never seen this one coming in a million years. Last year at this very same race I took second in my age and weight group. Only after the race when I was back at home did I discover from a friend that they had called my name at the awards ceremony. It was my first ever victory and I felt great.

Since that day, I had trained very hard to move up one podium position. It was the thought of sitting at the awards ceremony this year and getting the top podium position that motivated me when the alarm went off at 5 a.m. for all of those crazy early runs.

It was the thought of the awards ceremony photo as a "Thank you" to my sponsors and coach that kept me peddling after hour 10 of the triple bypass this year.

It was the thought of that magic moment that kept me swimming, cycling and running hard long after my weary body said to stop during the race. (BTW: I really surprised myself as I actually managed 22.5 mph average bike time during the race, which just happened to be four minutes slower than Michelle Jones.)

And it was that yearlong dream that I waited to fulfill as I sat in the boiling hot sun for over two hours waiting for the awards to be announced in Chicago on Sunday. Once again the Clydesdale division was last to be announced, but I waited because I knew I had won. Accenture had posted in on the Chicago Tri Web site and I got the confirmation via e-mail using their tracking systems.

So you can imagine how surprised I was when they announced the winner of my division and it was not me. It was a guy who went 2:40. I went 2:36 and beat last year's time by almost 4 minutes to take the top spot on the podium...except that somebody else got my medal, prize, and, moment in the sun, while I got nothing.

In fact when I asked the Capri race organizers about the mistake, they said nothing could be done. Those were the results they got from Timberline Timing and they would check into it. I pointed out the row of Accenture computers just a few feet away that had me (and have me listed) as the winner of my division, to no avail. They said they need to contact the timing company. I suggested that cell phones are plentiful and perhaps a phone call was in order to correct the mistake. They suggested I fill out a form and wait to hear from them.

On the empty-handed walk back to get my stuff out of transition, I wondered if this same mistake were to happen to a pro, would they just dismiss it so easily?

I wondered if they really cared about us big guys, us Everyman types, as much as they say. I wondered if they really cared about the age-group athletes who make up the bulk of their race and profits.

I wondered how the first and third place medal winners would feel when they checked the Web site results and figured out they were second and fourth.

They would certainly be surprised to be second and fourth.

But mostly I wondered how they had so casually snatched away the one moment that I had worked for this entire year. Sure they had said that if a mistake was made they would sort it out and order a new medal and send it to me.

But for me getting a medal in the mail six months later would hold little value. I wanted to thank all of my great sponsors with an awards ceremony photo, and I wanted that moment in the sun for myself.

But in the end I guess it just goes to show that no matter what you do,

even when you win,

there is always something that goes wrong at every race.

But please don't fret about me, I'm not taking it too hard. In the end, I'm just so very blessed that I have the friends, family, sponsors, and health to do this crazy sport.

In the big picture of life here in Boulder, this Everyman has every day in the sun.

There is always something...Ironman Wisconsin: The World's shortest race report

The Michelin Man Breaks 14 Hours in Madison

Note to self: shuffling a marathon is pretty much the same as run/walking it.

I want to thank my buddy Steve who came up from Chicago to support me during the race. A

guy could not ask for a better buddy.

Steve was there for me for the entire race, and he cheered me on as I stumbled through the run, and was with me from the stands as I took my last step across the finish line.

More importantly, he hung out with me as I sat on the bench and almost puked my guts out after the race, and he stayed with me until the very end as we cheered the last racers across the line.

For me the entire race was about bring out the best in people.

I am so very lucky to have:

- The best friends

- The best volunteers

- The best readers

- The best weather

- The best family

- The best sponsors

194

- The best day

I don't think I'll write a typical race report from the IM as it would be soooo boring. Plus, I'm not one for really getting into the minutia of my day like describing what I ate during the race. Nothing really went wrong, and that makes for a short report. You know something like this:

I woke up!

I put on tons of suntan lotion and body glide.

I swam, I biked, and I ran a hell of a long way.

I saw lots of great friends and incredible scenery.

Sometimes it was sunny, and sometimes it was cloudy.

Sometimes I was hot, and sometimes I was cold.

Sometimes I felt great, and sometimes I felt cruddy ... but mostly I felt happy to be alive and racing.

A few times people were cruddy, but most of the time they were great.

I ate and drank a whole bunch of silly stuff that somehow stayed down.

I crossed the finish line and tried to eat like a horse, but I couldn't.

I met my goal and still somehow managed the same run time, as not meeting my goal.

After the race I felt sick and cold, but better after I drank a coke.

I got tons of great congrats calls from my family and friends who wanted to know more details than I could process at the time.

I walked backwards up stairs and took a long ... long ... long ... hot shower.

I cheered and cried as the last finishers crossed the line.

I slept very hard.

I woke up and felt really sore and really content.

I took another long ... .long ... long hot shower and ate a huge breakfast, after which I ate another huge breakfast, after which I ate lunch.

And that's about all folks!

There is always something...Cheers and Jeers

Jeers: To the drunk college girl who came back from partying to our hotel at 2:30 a.m. and banged on everyone's door until she found her own room ... which just happened (as luck would have it) to be next to our room.

She proudly, and in a drunk voice, announced to her friends that she just woke up half of the hallway trying to find her room. Than she spent the next hour blabbing at top of her lungs until somebody finally screamed at her to "Shut the F" up in such a crazed homicidal manner that it even scared me.

I guess when you train an entire year for a race you probably want to get at least a few hours of sleep before the big day. I can see why you would happily take (say a chainsaw) to a rude and drunk coed who would think it funny to wake you up with her inane drunken blabbering at 3:30 a.m. At least that's what I was ready to do, had I a chainsaw and a few ounces of gas.

Cheers: To Scott from Fast Forward Sports and my buddy Steve for being two of the most excellent Sherpas. It was so nice to have them help me across the finish line at the end of the day.

Steve was kind enough to bring up his scooter from Chicago, which made the second loop of the bike so much easier. Scott was even kinder to take my number and chip and run a personal PR for me of 1:30 on the first half of the marathon.

You know I'm just kidding ... right?

These guys were terrific to me and it made my day that much more fun and special. I would highly recommend both of these fine fellows as your next race day Sherpas, and don't forget to tell Steve to bring his scooter..

Jeers: To the Mexican dude who took my run special needs bag.

In case you don't know you get two special needs bags for an IM. They give you these at the halfway point of the bike and of the marathon. I tend to put things like salt tablets, extra nutrition, and something like an ice tea to reward myself in these bags.

When I was in the transition area before the race checking on my transitions bags I put down my special needs bags for just a second. When I looked back my run special needs bag was gone.

I can only assume that the Mexican dude next to me picked it up thinking it was one of his. I only looked away for a few seconds and he was the only possible person who could have taken it, which is understandable since we are all carrying around a bunch of these bags. Only I wish he had put it into the special needs section for me since he must have known he had one too many bags.

In the end I had to beg and borrow salt tablets since I spilled all of mine on the bike, and my back-up stash never showed up for the run. And you know I was really looking forward to a sweet ice tea at hour 11 on the run.

That's a DQ

Photo by Wendy Buckner IM WI 2007

Jeers: To all of the swimmers I saw who cut the corners of the rectangle and swam inside the corner buoys, instead of outside the corner buoys. I saw at least several dozen people do this at each corner of the swim and it really made me angry.

I had a pretty crappy swim, as I was unable to make a clean single stroke without hitting somebody else. So I understand why hundreds of people swam inside the buoy line. That's all well and good, but you still need to come around, and not inside, the corner buoy.

Trust me, I completely understand why you would cut the corner. You are swimming along and in a few strokes you happen to be past the corner buoy, but on the inside of it.

I really get it, as a similar thing happened to me last week. I was sitting at home with a syringe full of EPO and before I knew it my hand slipped, and I had ejected myself with the stuff.

These things happen, right?

No they don't.

An Ironman swim is 2.4 mile and not 2.3 or 2.38. If you cut the corners for whatever reasons on the swim, in my book at least, you are not an Ironman. You are a DQed athlete.

Cheers: To all of the 3,500volunteers and thousands of spectators for helping out and coming to watch the race. I have never been to a more friendly race in my life. The entire weekend was like a magic carpet ride of joy and cheers. It was beyond my wildest expectations and I'll be forever in love with the fine folks of the city of Madison, Wisconsin.

Cheers: To Mike Ricci, my coach. Here's what he just wrote the team about me:

"Roman! - I don't know what Roman's goal was - but I knew he was going to do better than Great Floridian in 05. Two weeks ago, we tapered Roman for an OLY race, so I wasn't sure how he would handle the IM on an extended taper, but he did GREAT! Congrats Roman! Big guys can race fast too! Run splits: 2:43/2:49! Very nicely paced out Roman!"

So Mike needs to read my Blog ;-) but besides that I couldn't ask for better coach. He got me through the race in fine form. I felt great afterwards and I did exactly what I needed to do to be able to race this weekend. I had a huge smile on my face the entire day (except when I discovered my special needs bag was gone) and I completely blame Mike for that smile.

Thanks, Dude!

Jeers: To the guy on the bike course who gave me a dirty and disgusted look when I was on the phone to my wife and son in Colorado. I was coming up to the bike transition and I called, yes I called, my wife to tell her so that she and Tommy could see me on Ironman live when I came back from the bike. I also called her right before I crossed the finish line.

Dude, I'm not racing you for a Kona slot and the phone call was my only way of sharing the day with my family. So take a chill pill (preferably the suppository type) and relax. By that point in the race it must have been pretty obvious to anybody including you) that none of us was in the money, so just let me share my day with my family.

Cheers: To my family, friends, raceAthlete crew, readers, and great sponsors for all of your support this year. It was a great day. Thanks to all of you.

Cheers: To North American Sports for putting on a great race and for letting me get a voucher to register for next year before the race. I now have a gold ticket to next year's race, and best of all, I have until October 10 to register and pay.

Will I be racing again next year?

Photo by Wendy Buckner

I really can't say as of today, since I still have that half Ironman this weekend. We'll see, but I just having the gold ticket in my pocket makes me feel all giddy inside.

There is always something...Harvest Moon Triathlon

Do you want the good news, or the bad news first?

Let's start with the bad news.

As you may recall, flushed by my short course Clydesdale victory in Chicago, I registered for the Harvest Moon Half Ironman triathlon, as it is the long course Clydesdale & Athena National Championships. It was also a week after Ironman Wisconsin.

The bad news is, the wheels pretty much came off the cart at about mile eight on the run. I got to a point yesterday when I had nothing in the tank.

Often times you'll hear people use that expression "nothing in the tank" to express a feeling of weakness and general fatigue. In fact, I believe I've used the expression myself when referring to my typical race bonk.

This felt nothing like that. I literally had nothing, no fumes, drips, no reserve left in the tank. I was completely on empty. The only thing that kept me going was the knowledge that I was in the lead and a herd, pack, gaggle, school, or whatever you'd call a big group of Clydesdales was running up my behind.

I know this because it was an out and back half marathon so it was pretty easy to know who was ahead, and more importantly, who was behind me.

With five miles left to go, I was barely holding on to perhaps a 5-to-10 minute lead on the next big guy in my division.

The fact that the wheels came off my cart with such a slim lead on the run is Part One of the bad news.

The good news is that you guys were completely wrong about how much pain I'd feel doing half IM just a week a full IM. I can honestly say that I felt no more or less pain than a usual race. I guess I was lucky with the nutrition as this was not an issue.

Normally the worst pain comes when you get that part wrong because there really is nothing like heaving out your guts on mile two of a half or full marathon. Now that's a barrel of monkeys when it comes to sheer pain and endurance.

But yesterday for me, at least in terms of pain, was really no different from any other half IM I've ever raced. I had the same high and lows, the same struggle to keep running when I felt like I could not take another step, the same butt burn on the bike, and the same apprehension before the start as I waded into the chilly cold waters of the swim.

It was like any other race with one huge exception. I really had no top gear when I need one.

In other words, image that your body is like a car and you have five gears. You can think of them as five heart rate zones if that's easier to conceptualize. Normally when you race, you tend to switch gears ... sometimes on purpose and sometimes without your conscious knowledge.

For instance, you may switch to a higher gear at the start of the swim to get away from the flying arms and feet of the typical mass triathlon start. You may switch to a higher gear on the bike when climbing, you may switch to a lower gear when descending.

I often will switch into a higher gear at the end of the bike without really knowing it. You know, you can smell the hay in the barn and boy do you want to be in that barn (transition area).

On the run the same thing happens to many of us when we see and hear the finish line.

Yesterday, no matter how hard I tried I could not get past 3rd gear. Fourth and fifth gears were completely off the menu. My body would not shift into any higher gear past 3rd … period.

That's the bad news.

The good news is I felt really comfortable in third gear. I think I could have gone all day in the water and on the bike in 3rd gear. And the really good news is that for 95 percent of the time in a long course triathlon you don't need the 4th or 5th gear.

The bad news is that when you do need them … like when you are at the end of the race and you are tied in a head to head battle for first in your division … they are good gears to have.

Yesterday was such a day. I was able to use third gear for almost the entire race and do really well. But when I needed those extra gears, I didn't have them.

The really, really good news is that I think I took second in my division!

I'm not sure, as once again I was robbed of the awards ceremony and photo opportunity. This time the weather intervened. As is almost always the case, they left the Clydesdale and Athena awards for last. By the time they got to us, a massive thunderstorm rolled in and all hell broke loose. The wind picked up, the rain came down in sheets, and the awards were canceled.

I asked the race director if I could have my award and he said, "No way! We'll mail it to you."

And that was that.

Once again I left empty-handed, plus cold, and wet.

Please don't get me wrong, I'm not complaining. At least I was done with my race, and not out in the storm and cold with the many brave age groupers still fighting to cross the finish line.

I'm only guessing that I took second in my division from my race,as it looked that way from the results that were posted after the race. But these are not official, and as I write this the results have yet to be posted on the race Web site.

So here I sit with what I know is a first place finish in Chicago and what I think is a second place finish yesterday and I have nothing to show for it except the knowledge that I raced as hard as I could have raced on both days.

And you know what? Surprisingly that's enough. The folks at Capri Events have yet to send me anything a full three weeks after the Chicago Triathlon, and I really don't have official notification of anything from yesterday's race.

I only have the knowledge that after an entire summer of training and training and training, I did the very best I could at the two races that meant the most to me.

There is no doubt in my mind that I could not have gone a smidgen faster yesterday. It took me a few minutes over six hours.

There is no doubt in my mind that I could not have gone a smidgen faster at the Chicago Triathlon.

In both races I raced as hard as I could have. I think for us age-groupers that's the ultimate prize for success. It is the personal victory that holds the most meaning. The knowledge that on race day we showed up and gave it our all.

Sure, sometimes life gets in the way of our training, or family and friends come well ahead of our amateur triathlon careers. Unlike the pros, we don't get paid, and most of the time we certainly don't end up winning our age-groups. So that leaves us with the knowledge that we came and gave it our all.

And I'm really good with that.

BTW: I looked at my time from last year's Harvest Moon Triathlon and it was about 15 minutes faster. But that's really meaningless, as this year they changed the bike and run course in a very substantial way. They added a lot more hills to both, so this year was much tougher.

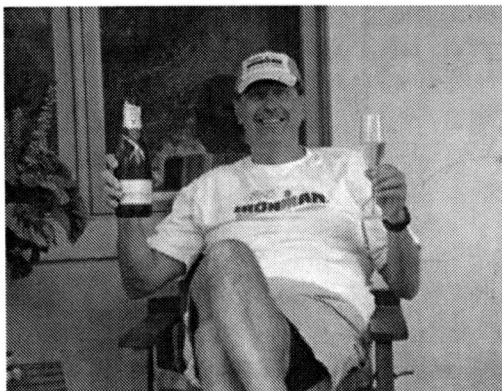

Could I have taken first place had I not done Ironman Wisconsin last week?

It's a meaningless question, as my results are what they are.

Would I recommend doing an Olympic, half IM, and a full Ironman in one month? The Everyman hat trick?

That's something I can't really say right now. The fact is that you can't perform at the top of your game in that many races in that short of a time.

You end up making some serious compromises and your performance suffers.

The good news is that you guys came along with me on this crazy journey. I thank you for sharing it with me.

And the really good news is: I'm done for this year, and now I get to dream about racing next year ... Oh yes, and eat a really big lunch today!

Breinigsville, PA USA
22 March 2010
234647BV00002B/11/A